The author of *The Child Within* writes:

"I was in the fifth month of pregnancy when I experienced the trauma of miscarriage. Lying on my bed, staring into the still darkness of midnight, I prayed that the stabbing contractions would stop, that the child within me would be safe.

"I was alone when the miscarriage happened—and yet, I was not alone...."

BEYOND HEARTACHE

MARI HANES
with
Jack Hayford

LIVING BOOKS
Tyndale House Publishers, Inc.
Wheaton, Illinois

All Scripture references are taken from the
King James Version (KJV) and *The Living Bible
(TLB),* unless otherwise noted.

First printing, March 1984

Library of Congress Catalog Card Number 83-51447
ISBN 0-8423-0135-6
Copyright © 1984 by Mari Hanes
Printed in the United States of America

CONTENTS

FOREWORD

I was in the fifth month of pregnancy when I experienced the trauma of miscarriage. Lying on my bed, staring into the still darkness of midnight, I prayed that the stabbing contractions would stop, that the child within me would be safe. For ten days I had been bleeding and feeling these pains. *Maybe,* I thought hopefully, *this is false labor.* But the labor was real, and I had waited too long to drive to the hospital.

I was alone when the miscarriage happened —and yet, I was not alone. The Word of God was there, and promises of Scripture surrounded me as if they were inscribed on the bedroom walls. I was in pain, but not terrified; I was grieving, but "not as they who have no hope." I prayed, knowing with certainty that the prayer was ushering my baby into the presence of the heavenly Father.

Because I had studied Scripture concerning the unborn infant when I was writing *The Child Within*, my husband and I were sustained by peace. Later that week our friend Pastor Jack Hayford sent us a teaching cassette entitled "Short-circuit into Eternity: A study of the destiny of miscarried or aborted infants." My heart had already been greatly moved by letters from women who had read *The Child Within* and had questions about miscarriage. Following the loss of my own child during pregnancy, I determined to provide young mothers with the scriptural certainty of what their grieving hearts hope for. I also wanted to establish the fact of the reality of life before birth, as well as the eternal aspect of that life.

This book has been written for couples in several different categories. I pray it will give biblical insight and comfort to those who have lost children through miscarriage, stillbirth, abortion, or placing a child for adoption. The book also includes thoughts for couples struggling with the problems of infertility.

Most of all, I hope to encourage readers to move into a ministry of comforting others; as Isaiah urges, "Comfort ye my people. . . ." At least 300,000 women each year suffer the trauma of miscarriage. Many more have stillborn infants.

In 1980, there were around 1,300,000 legal abortions. That figure does not include many illegal ones. Much is being said in Christian circles about the sin of abortion, and rightly so, but at least one out of every eight American women of child-bearing age has *already* had one. Many of these women have since become Christians, and yet no book deals with the emotional healing and forgiveness available to women who live in regret.

How are we to live? Certainly not "as those who have no hope." May faith sustain you, faith in the name of the One who is our Hope.

Mari Hanes

 LETTERS
FROM
HURTING
WOMEN

Dear Mari,

I read your book *The Child Within* during my first pregnancy, and gave birth to a healthy eight-pound baby girl. Since that time I have gone through two miscarriages. The last miscarriage was a nightmare because I carried the child almost full term before my doctor discovered that the baby had died. I had to carry the child for two more weeks, knowing that it was dead inside of me, before they finally induced labor.

I am trying to have faith, but I'll admit that I'm dealing with some bitterness. Miscarriage and stillbirth seem so pointless, so unfair. At first I thought that I would go crazy.

Do you know of any verses of Scripture that might be a comfort to me at this time? And will you please pray for me that I will be able to find the courage to try again?

Waiting to hear from you,
Anne

Dear Pastor Jack,

I am twenty-three years old, but I am still suffering from something that happened to me when I was fifteen. . . .

I got pregnant by a boy that I really cared about, but when I told him I was carrying his child, he split. I was afraid to tell my folks or my sister or anyone. I kept hoping that he would come back to town and marry me, but he never did. I just didn't know what to do, so for a long time I just did nothing.

Finally in my fifth month I knew I couldn't hide the pregnancy any longer, so I went in for an abortion. I didn't know if I could even get one by that time, but with a little talking and with three doctors giving consent, the hospital said OK.

Because I wasn't showing much on the outside, I guess I just didn't realize how big and fully formed that baby would be. No one warned me what a horrible ordeal that abortion would be. No one told me that I wouldn't be totally unconscious, or that my mind would carry such clear and awful memories of that day. . . . As soon as it was over, I was so filled with regret that I didn't know what to do.

Then last year I became a Christian, and now I believe that that fetus was an eternal soul. Do you believe that it was? Pastor Jack, I really love the Lord, but I just don't see how he can love me. With all of my heart, I just wish that I could feel forgiven. . . .

Thank you for listening to me.

Love,
Janet

Dear Mari,

Three years ago, when I was sixteen, I had a baby boy and I gave him up for adoption. At the time I felt it was the wisest decision and the best thing that I could do for him. I received good counsel from good people, and they thought that in my case adoption was right. I guess I still believe that it was right. But I have been wondering, "What does God think?"

Is there anything in the Bible about adoption? Do you think that God is unhappy with a woman who bears a child and then gives it away?

I have heard what people think, but I really want to know what God thinks. . . .

Please answer soon,
Tiffany

Dear Pastor Jack,

I have heard you teach several times on the blessings of having children. My husband Ted and I agree with everything that you say, but to hear teachings like this always brings us deep heartaches. We have been trying to conceive a child for our entire seven years of marriage, and so far have not been able to have a baby.

What counsel do you have for couples in our situation? We are getting so desperate that we're even ready to consider a surrogate mother. We really value your opinion. More than anything, we want to find out what God's will is for our situation.

Sincerely and prayerfully,
Darlene and Ted

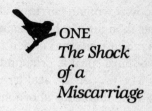

ONE
The Shock of a Miscarriage

Jesus the Son of God is our great High Priest who has gone to heaven itself to help us; therefore let us never stop trusting him. This High Priest of ours understands our weaknesses. . . .

For we have not an high priest which cannot be touched with the feeling of our infirmities. . . . Hebrews 4:14, 15, TLB, KJV

Words cannot accurately describe the aching emptiness that a woman feels immediately after having a miscarriage.

Her body screams to her that it is no longer pregnant. Jolted back to an unpregnant state, it works to normalize hormone levels and the entire reproductive system. For weeks her physical form has been "home" for someone else. Now internal organs such as the pituitary gland flood her body with one message: "vacant."

For most women, the emptiness is far more than physical. Besides carrying a child in her body, a woman carries a child in her heart. In her thoughts. In her dreams. When that child is miscarried, the sudden emptiness in a woman's spirit is profound.

The proper medical term for a miscarriage is a "spontaneous abortion." This term usually applies to any fetus delivered unliving in the first two trimesters of pregnancy. In the last trimester, the delivery of a deceased infant is termed a "stillbirth." To the woman whose child is stillborn comes the most overwhelming emptiness of all.

It is amazing that so little information is available on the subject of miscarriage, considering that over 300,000 American women go through this experience each year. Current studies from the Center for Disease Control in Atlanta, Georgia, reveal that roughly one in five conceptions ends in a miscarriage. This means that a very large number of women have to deal with this heartache at some point in their childbearing years. If your heart has been torn because of a spontaneous abortion, you are not alone.

It is also amazing that so little has been offered by way of scriptural comfort to couples who find themselves in this situation, for the

Word of God is laced with many wonderful truths concerning the unborn child.

THE EMOTIONAL AFTERMATH

The actual experience of a miscarriage is as varied and unique as are the women who go through this tragedy. Some expectant mothers have almost no warning signals, and are shocked to discover they are hemorrhaging. Other women who have experienced live births testify that the labor of a miscarriage can be just as severe and intense as the labor and delivery of a large, full-term infant.

Because the medical experience of miscarriage is so diversified, this book deals basically with the emotional aftermath, rather than the medical aftermath, of a spontaneous abortion. The emotional aftermath usually follows a specific pattern.

The initial response to a miscarriage is one of *shock* and *bewilderment*. A miscarriage is one of life's great disappointments. Though some women have many days of warning due to cramping and spotting, others miscarry suddenly with little or no previous signs. Psychologists tell us that in a trauma for which we have little time to prepare, our mental and emotional reactions are delayed.

Many women who have suffered a spontaneous abortion report that following the first

stage of physical shock, they found themselves
going through a time of emotional "numbness,"
of being "in a daze." You may, for a short time,
find yourself unable to *respond*—to your
husband, to friends, or even to the Lord. It is as
if the well of your heart has been drained dry.

Next may come a feeling, however brief, of
calmness and *relief.* There is an actual medical
term for this sensation: the "survival syndrome." This feeling is simply your body's
response to the fact that the physical pain of
the event is over. During the miscarriage you
were probably very much afraid. Now it is
over, and you realize that you have not been
physically harmed. You have "survived."

Then, after a few days, most women move
into the fourth stage: the troubling time of
questioning, of *self-doubt,* even of *self-imposed
guilt.* This fourth stage can last for weeks, even
months. If not faced and resolved, the guilt-
ridden questioning can bring torment for years.

A woman can be extremely hard on herself
following a miscarriage. She may try to put the
blame on something she did or did not do. She
may wonder:

Was I on my feet too much?

Maybe I didn't eat enough of the right foods.

Maybe the antibiotic I took when I caught
that cold caused this to happen.

Maybe I was under too much pressure at the
office.

Although this book deals with the emotional rather than the physical facts of a miscarriage, there is one medical fact which, when understood, will have a great impact on your emotions—emotions which often center around the ever-present question: "Why did I have this miscarriage?"

The simple medical fact which applies to many of the children lost in the first trimester and to a great number of those miscarried later is that *something was wrong with the fetus.*

A woman who has just gone through a spontaneous abortion often feels a great surge of guilt, albeit sometimes vague and unnamed. Somehow, deep in her heart, she is saying, *"This must have been my fault."* The plain medical truth is that a miscarriage is most often "the delivery of a premature fetus that would not be normal and could not live on its own."

The more that scientists learn about the field of genetics, the more amazed they become that chromosomes can actually come together perfectly and that trillions of cells can form properly to produce a healthy human being. The number of possibilities for something to go wrong is endless, yet the vast majority of all babies develop with *complex perfection!*

The most recent medical studies seem to indicate that if a fetus does begin to develop improperly, it actually sends out messages to a woman's body, telling it that things are not right and commanding a spontaneous abortion. Most of the events which cause genetic abnormalities in the fetus occur during chromosome division or migration, and thus are not the result of genetic problems inherited from the parents.

Geneticists tell us that nature has written these messages into the fetal system so that the mother is spared the anguish of bearing a severely deformed or weakened infant. As Christians, we can see that God, in his divine mercy, wove this law into nature. It is, to quote a phrase made familiar by Sheldon Vanauken, a "severe mercy."

If your physician tells you there was no apparent reason for your miscarriage, he probably feels that the problem was an *improperly developing fetus*. You did not cause the miscarriage; you must reject the burden of false guilt.

Do you experience feelings of condemnation about the miscarriage and about other situations? At the root of condemnation are emotional and mental lies. The verses at the end of this chapter identify the source of those lies. It is only as you reject false guilt that you can move through the last stage of this season of grieving.

If you have had more than one spontaneous abortion, your doctor may begin to consider other possibilities. These include:

a. anatomical abnormalities: an imperfect development of the uterus or vagina, adhesions inside the uterus, or *myomas.*

b. infections, especially within the uterus itself: *T-strain mycoplasmas,* for example.

c. hormonal, or immunological disorders.

d. a small possibility of harm from drugs or chemicals.

Note: Except for a severe injury during pregnancy, such as from an automobile accident, there is no reason to believe that a miscarriage was caused by accidental trauma (from a fall, for example) to the abdomen.

It will be wise in the future to deal with any possible cause of harm in a pregnancy, and to use all available spiritual and medical knowledge (this will be discussed further in later chapters). But for now, your task is to lay aside self-examination and guilt; otherwise, you will never be able to deal with your depression and disappointment.

Now we come to the final stage of the emotional aftermath: *dealing with your heartache and great disappointment.* Later in this book we will try to answer the questions asked most often, questions such as "How long will I feel the grief?" and "How can I keep from feeling bitter?" But even now you must begin to make some choices. You need to ask yourself some in-depth questions:

"Will I allow this experience to draw me and my husband closer, or will I allow the emotional pressure to build walls between us?"

"Will I receive the support offered by friends and relatives, or will I choose to be closed and withdrawn?"

"Will I begin to overcome this emotional trauma, or will I live in fear of future pregnancies?"

The Word of God can give you wonderfully practical, heart-healing advice at this time. Just as at all other times of your life, Scripture will give you more than solid counsel. It will give you fresh hope and a wellspring of deep inner strength.

GOD'S COMPASSION

More than at any other time in your life, you need to be convinced that God really cares about you. First John 4:9, 10 and Romans 10:9 show the greatest way in which he has said, "I really love you." He demonstrated his love by laying down his life.

God the Father extends his love to you at this time like a priceless gift. Romans 10:9 gives the powerful simplicity of how this gift of love is received: "If thou shalt confess with thy mouth the Lord Jesus, and shalt believe in thine heart that God hath raised him from the dead, thou shalt be saved" *(KJV)*.

The Lord Jesus not only loves you—he understands you perfectly. This is possible because he became "flesh, and dwelt among us" (John 1:14, *KJV*). In Isaiah 42:14, we learn that God even understands what it is to feel "labor pains" as he labors to bring spiritual children to life! Luke 13:34 and Matthew 23:37 also show that he understands a mother's heart.

DEALING WITH FALSE GUILT

Someone may have thoughtlessly made a statement such as "You were on your feet too much during your pregnancy, and that could have caused the miscarriage."

But what does God's Word tell us about "old wives' tales"? First Timothy 4:7 urges us to avoid all vain superstition.

Even without the troubling words of others, you may be condemning yourself. In John 8:44, Jesus tells us the source of false, unreasonable guilt. He says, "Satan is a liar, and the father of lies" *(New International Version)*.

Our spiritual enemy often tries to place untrue thoughts in our minds. Have you experienced any "lies" since the miscarriage (any condemning thoughts about what you should or should not have done during your pregnancy)?

If you have been bombarded by false guilt, you may wish to memorize Romans 8:1: "There is therefore now no condemnation to them which are in Christ Jesus" *(KJV)*. Another portion of Scripture which you should memorize and treasure in your heart is Psalm 103:8, 14.

DRAWING ON DIVINE PROVISION

A miscarriage hardly ever affects your health or the health of any baby you may carry in the future. But if you need physical healing, there are scriptural promises for you to claim:

1. Healing for the "miscarrying" womb (tipped uterus, etc.):

May the God of your fathers, the Almighty, bless you with blessings of heaven above and of the earth beneath—blessings of the breasts *and of the womb* (Genesis 49:25, TLB).

Children are a gift from God; they are his reward (Psalm 127:3, TLB).

2. Healing for infection or internal problems:

 . . . The earnest prayer of a righteous man has great power and wonderful results (James 5:16, TLB).

But he was wounded and bruised for our *sins. He was chastised that we might have peace; he was lashed—and we were healed!* (Isaiah 53:5, TLB).

He forgives all my sins. He heals me (Psalm 103:3, TLB).

3. Health for future children:

He gives children to the childless wife, so that she becomes a happy mother . . . (Psalm 113:9, TLB).

Your wife shall be contented in your home. And look at all those children! There they sit around the dinner table as vigorous and healthy as young olive trees (Psalm 128:3, TLB).

CONCLUSION

There are myriad physical and emotional experiences connected with a spontaneous abortion. In whatever state you find yourself, there is the Comforter, the Friend who is "closer than a brother," the High Priest who can be touched and who understands your thoughts and feelings.

Even if you know for certain that the fetus you miscarried was malformed or deficient, any lost pregnancy can seem so futile, so meaningless. This is especially true for those who believe life is purely physical. But as a

Christian, you understand a deeper truth: the reality of the soul and the spirit.

Since you believe this, the pressing questions on your heart are "At what point does a fetus possess an eternal soul?" and "Do I have a child in heaven?"

The answers are clearly dealt with in Scripture. Knowledge of the Word always brings us hope, and in this case that hope will keep the painful experience of miscarriage from being so meaningless. "For I know the plans I have for you, says the Lord. They are plans for good and not for evil, to give you a future and a hope" (Jeremiah 29:11, *TLB*).

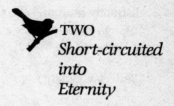

TWO
Short-circuited into Eternity

But I would not have you to be ignorant, brethren, concerning them which are asleep, that ye sorrow not, even as others which have no hope.

Which hope we have as an anchor of the soul, both sure and steadfast. . . . 1 Thessalonians 4:13 and Hebrews 6:19, KJV

Every woman who has suffered a miscarriage wonders if the embryo or fetus was a human soul with eternal potential. Almost everyone, when asked if she believes that the fetus is now in heaven with the Father, will reply, "I think so. I really do think so. . . ." And you respond, "If only I could know for sure!"

Is an embryo a human life, even in the earliest weeks after conception? Is it a human life with an *eternal soul*?

Is it a human life?
"Yes!" say biologists.

"From their first hour, the human cells are distinctly human," according to *The Position of Modern Science on the Beginning of Human Life.*

"Yes!" say geneticists.

"I will maintain the utmost respect for human life from the time of conception," as stated in the *Proceedings of the Fourth International Congress on Human Genetics* (Paris, 1971).

"Yes!" say fetologists.

" . . . The fetus is not a passive, dependent, nerveless, fragile vegetable as tradition has held, but a young human being, dynamic, resilient, and in a very large measure in charge of his environment" cited from *the Foetus in Charge of His Environment* by A. W. Liley.

But, is this a human life with an *eternal soul?*
Yes! This fact is clearly stated in our textbook of eternal life—the Bible. Scripture has much to say about the *prenatal existence of the human soul.*

Many of the men whose stories are recorded in the Bible were touched by the Holy Spirit *before* they were born. In Jeremiah 1:5, God spoke to the prophet Jeremiah and said, "Before I formed thee in the belly I knew thee; and before thou camest forth out of the womb I sanctified thee" *(KJV)*. From Isaiah 49:1 we learn that "the Lord called me before my birth. From within the womb he called me by name" *(TLB)*. In the New Testament, the Apostle Paul says, "For even before I was born God had chosen me to be his and called me—what kindness and grace" (Galatians 1:15, *TLB*).

The Gospel of Luke has a tremendous passage on the spirit of the unborn child. Included in the Gospel by divine purpose is a conversation between two expectant mothers, Elizabeth and Mary.

In Luke 1:12 the angel Gabriel announces that John the Baptist will be *filled* with the Holy Spirit while he is yet in the womb of Elizabeth. Later in that chapter, Mary arrives for a visit in the home of Elizabeth and Zacharias. In verse 41, Elizabeth's unborn son, John, *leaps for joy,* demonstrating an unfathomable spiritual and emotional response, when he hears the sound of Mary's salutation.

John the Baptist is to have a ministry which announces the coming of the Messiah, and actually makes his first "announcement" before his birth!

In this same passage, Elizabeth greets Mary with the words, "What an honor this is, that the mother of my Lord should visit me!" We know from the chronology given that Mary is only three or four weeks pregnant at this time. By prophetic utterance, Elizabeth recognizes that the tiny life in Mary's womb is already the Messiah. She does not say, "You will be the mother of my Lord." She says, "You *are* the mother of my Lord."

Skeptics say, "It seems unbelievable that an embryo can possess spirit and soul in the early days of pregnancy. *When exactly does a human receive his spirit?*" As believers, we need to realize that this is a *wrong question.* A human being *is* spirit, soul, and body—three elements meshed into one.

It is interesting to note that in this chapter from Luke the words "unborn child" (referring to John the Baptist) are translated from the Greek word *brephos,* used to describe Jesus in Luke 2:12 as "the babe wrapped in swaddling clothes" *(KJV).* In the original scriptural text, no distinction was made between an unborn child and a newborn child.

One of the Bible's most graphic pictures of the unborn child is found in Psalm 139:13-16, which says, "You made all the delicate, inner parts of my body, and knit them together in my mother's womb. Thank you for making me so wonderfully complex! It is amazing to think about. Your workmanship is marvelous—and how well I know it. You were there when I was being formed in utter seclusion! You saw me before I was born . . . before I began to breathe" *(TLB).*

The *King James Version* renders these words of King David as "Thou hast possessed my reins. . . ." In Hebrew, the word for "reins" means "the seat of human affection" or "the foundation of my being."

These portions of Scripture, along with those given throughout the book, will give you hope in the midst of your pain. Your tiny baby was not a mere collection of cells, but a *spiritual being.* Further scriptural study assures us that each miscarried fetus has a positive eternal destiny.

A look at Job 3:9-19 will shed light on this fact. In the midst of great trial for a time, Job is so distressed that he says, "I wish I had never been born!" He goes on to provide us with a lesson about the destiny of babies which are miscarried. In verse sixteen he says, "Oh, that I had been an *untimely birth,* as an *infant which never saw the light.* . . ." Then he goes on to give his reason:

" . . . Then had I been at rest with kings and counselors of the earth . . . with princes that had gold, that filled their houses with silver. . . . There the wicked cease from troubling; and there the weary be at rest. There the prisoners rest together; they hear not the voice of the oppressor. The small and great are there. . . ."

Job is speaking of those who never saw the light of the sun on this planet (verse 16), but who are eternal beings nonetheless—eternal beings who were, in a manner of speaking, short-circuited into eternity. (A parallel Scripture is Jeremiah 20:17.)

Ecclesiastes 6:3-5 is yet another example of the positive destiny of children short-circuited into eternity: "If a man beget an hundred children, and live many years, so that the days of his life be many, and his soul be not filled with good . . . I say, that an untimely birth is better than he. . . . Moreover he hath not seen the sun, nor known any thing: this hath more rest than the other."

You may be one of the thousands who have experienced a miscarriage and cried, "Oh, I hope that tiny fetus was a whole person in God's eyes; and that I will see that child in the life to come!" You can now say with confidence, "I *will* see that child in eternity."

There is another question in the hearts of those who believe their miscarried infants are now in heaven in the presence of the Lord: *What quality of existence will the miscarried life have in heaven?*

A true understanding of what heaven and eternity will be like is totally beyond our comprehension at this time. But a relatively recent scientific discovery places tremendous significance in what the Bible has said all along, and points the way to a probable answer to this question.

DNA. *Deoxyribonucleic acid.* A few years ago this nucleic acid was totally unknown. But in 1953 in Cambridge, England, two scientists discovered and studied the fundamental molecule of life. Every normal human cell (including each cell of an embryo from the moment of conception) contains forty-six chromosomes—genetic material. Half of this material has been provided by the father and half by the mother. DNA is located along the chromosomes of each cell, and takes the form of a kind of microscopic spiral staircase.

Conceptually, DNA is a tiny computer, miniaturized beyond Sony's wildest dreams. ... Programmed into this data bank is an almost inconceivable amount of information that spells out the biological and chemical functions of life. A single thread of DNA located in just one human cell may house as much information as *one thousand books,* each six hundred pages thick.

Such detailed information will determine everything from the color of a baby's eyes to the height he will reach at maturity!

We have already looked at Psalm 139:16, in

The Living Bible. The *King James Version* puts it this way: "Thine eyes did see my substance, yet being unperfect; and in thy book all my members were written, which in continuance were fashioned, when as yet there was none of them."

What a profound statement! In identifying chromosomes and defining DNA, modern geneticists have looked into their microscopes and discovered God's "book," or blueprint, with complete instructions for the construction of an individual human being!

It is reasonable and entirely logical to believe that in heaven, the Master Architect takes the blueprint from the cells of a miscarried infant and simply completes the construction of what was already in process.

One final question remains: Will you be able to recognize your child in heaven?

There are examples in Scripture of men who had gone to be with the Lord and were recognizable even to those who had never seen them (see Matthew 17—the Mount of Transfiguration). In speaking of the perfection of eternity, the Apostle Paul says, "For now I know in part; but then I shall know even as also I am known" (1 Corinthians 13:12, *KJV*).

King David lost a child at birth. In 2 Samuel 12:23 *(KJV),* this man of faith said, "I shall go to him, but he shall not return to me." David was clearly planning to recognize his son.

Understanding what the Word of God has to say about children who are "short-circuited" into eternity will not completely erase the emotional pain of a miscarriage. But it will prevent you from sorrowing "as those sorrow who have no hope." Your miscarriage was not a pointless trial. You now have a great investment in the heavenly kingdom.

MOVING THROUGH YOUR SORROW

In times of great grieving, believers often wish that Jesus Christ were physically present on this earth, walking with them as he once walked with the disciples. Yet in John 16:7 *(KJV)*, Jesus said, "It is expedient for you [or 'to your advantage'] that I go away." Why? Jesus said that when he returned to the Father, the Comforter would come: "The Comforter, which is the Holy Ghost, whom the Father will send in my name, he shall teach you all things, and bring all things to your remembrance, whatsoever I have said unto you. Peace I leave with you. . . . Let not your heart be troubled, neither let it be afraid" (John 14:26, 27, *KJV*).

The Greek word for "Comforter" is *Paracletos*. A *paraclete* is literally "one called alongside to help." In the hard times of life, the days of questioning, of weeping, of weakness, you can sense God's Spirit at your side, supporting and upholding you, giving you divine strength.

FOR FURTHER STUDY

"The Ministry of the Holy Spirit":
The following references describe the work of the Holy Spirit.

1. Isaiah 61:1—He has sent us to heal.
2. Luke 11:13—He is a gift from the loving Father.
3. John 14:26—He comforts us.
4. John 16:13—He instructs in wisdom.
5. Acts 1:8—He gives power to face life.
6. Galatians 4:6—He draws us close to the Father.

"Descriptions of the Joy of Eternity":
The following verses will comfort you.

1. 1 Corinthians 2:9 *(KJV):* "Eye hath not seen, nor ear heard, neither have entered into the heart of man, the things which God hath prepared for them that love him."

2. Isaiah 11:6 *(TLB):* "In that day the wolf and the lamb will lie down together, and the leopard and goats will be at peace. Calves and fat cattle will be safe among lions, and a little child shall lead them all."

(See also: Psalm 31:19; Isaiah 25:8; Matthew 25:34; 1 Corinthians 15:24; and 2 Corinthians 5:7.)

ANOTHER LOOK

In the field of electricity, there is a standard circuit, or pathway, along which the current travels before returning to its source. To say that something is short-circuited means that a connection of relatively low resistance was accidentally made between the points in an electric circuit. In calling this chapter "Short-circuited into Eternity," I am saying that though a miscarried life travels an unusual pathway, the flow of that life is never lost. It completely bypasses life on this earth, returning to its source, the Creator.

In talking to married couples who have experienced miscarriage, Pastor Jack Hayford has found the following counsel to be helpful:

1. Pray a simple prayer, presenting the little one to the Lord. (Presenting, or dedicating, children to the Lord is entirely scriptural. See Luke 2:22-35 regarding Jesus' dedication.)

2. Consider choosing a name for the miscarried child and privately treasure that knowledge between you and your spouse.

3. Look forward to meeting that child someday, knowing you have a great investment in the heavenly kingdom.

Pastor Hayford comments:

"It is only my opinion, but I believe that we may even have the marvelous opportunity to share with the children who never walked on this earth how it was to walk in rebellion to the Creator, and then be restored to him through faith in Christ Jesus."

There are many days when the richness of life on earth so fills our hearts that we cannot comprehend that heaven could compare with the present. Yet in the days when we see the flaws in the present, when we feel the heart-break caused by death and our present physical imperfection, we look with hope to the age described in Isaiah 65:17, 20, 23: "For, behold, I create new heavens and a new earth. . . . No longer will babies die when only a few days old; no longer will men be considered old at 100! They shall not labour in vain, nor bring forth for trouble. For they are the children of those the Lord has blessed, and their children, too, shall be blessed" *(KJV and TLB).*

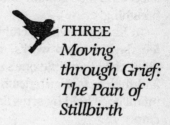

THREE
Moving through Grief: The Pain of Stillbirth

*Then David arose from the earth, and washed,
and anointed himself, and changed his
apparel, and came into the house of the Lord,
and worshipped. . . . And he said, While the
child was yet alive, I fasted and wept. . . .
But now he is dead, wherefore should I fast?
Can I bring him back again? I shall go to him,
but he shall not return to me.*

*. . . Ye know that your labour is not in vain
in the Lord.* 2 Samuel 12:20, 22, 23 and
1 Corinthians 15:58, KJV

To carry a baby for nine long months, to go to
the hospital happily confident, to travail
through hours of labor, only finally to
experience the unexpected anguish of a stillbirth. . . .

To deliver a premature infant, to spend days at the hospital nursery watching that one fight to survive and struggle to develop, and then to see him lose ground and suddenly stop breathing. . . .

To have a newborn child in your home for a few days or a few weeks, to experience and appreciate that little one's unique personality, and then to face crib death and to miss that infant once held by arms that are now achingly empty. . . .

Moments such as these bring a depth of grieving that cannot be put into words.

Attempts from friends and family to comfort you seem trite and shallow. Your home feels dark and vacant. Faith can be almost devastated.

King David experienced a similar anguish— the death of a newborn son—yet his faith was not shaken. He was able to enter the presence of the Lord and worship him. King David was able to declare with confidence, "He shall not return to me, but I shall go to him." It was at that point that David was strong enough to minister comfort to his grieving wife.

How? What knowledge would enable a brokenhearted parent to have that reaction? Was King David superhuman, a man of such spiritual strength that he wasn't chained to the normal feelings of the flesh?

No. David was not superspiritual. His entire

life is recorded accurately in the Bible so we can see that he was just like us; very human, very vulnerable. King David viewed death as an enemy. When he lost his son, he could go to the Lord in worship because he knew that God had a plan to overcome that enemy. In Psalm 49:15 he wrote, "God will redeem my soul from the power of the grave" *(KJV)*.

Christians have sometimes tried to soften the impact of death, speaking as though each death is sent from God, talking of "crossing the Jordan," or trying to portray death as a friend that conveys us from this troubled world into the world of eternity. Maybe somehow it has been implied that this is a "spiritual" view of death. But you do not have to see death as anything less than it really is—the enemy that took your infant and left you such emotional pain.

Jesus did not paint a rosy picture of death nor call it a friend. He saw death as an enemy to battle on *our* behalf. In fact, he wept because of the grief that physical death brings to a family (see John, chapter 11).

Scripture tells us that the Son of God came to destroy all the works of darkness, that "the last Enemy which shall be destroyed is death." Jesus came in the flesh to regain for mankind the "keys of death" (Revelation 1:18).

Death is, in reality, painful separation. Because of the sickness and the decay which are in the world through sin, death has come to claim mankind and bring eternal separation between you and your Creator, between you and your loved ones. But through his finished work on the cross, Christ can now override the claims of sin on mankind and, therefore, override death. When death stretches out a chilling hand to steal away a life, Christ's strong grasp of love overrules the grasp of destruction. "No, Death," he says, "this eternal soul is mine!"

This is why 1 Corinthians 15:55 says, "O death, where is thy sting?" As you consider the loss of your infant, realize that at the very moment in which physical problems caused his body to stop functioning, the Lord claimed that little one as his own with authority that superseded the claims of death.

The Scriptures covered in chapter two give assurance of the eternal destiny of the stillborn child or the miscarried infant. Well acquainted with the promises of God, King David was certain that the future held an eternity of fellowship with his son. But he was also able to worship in the midst of grief, because he understood that God's plan for eternity involves not just a *quantity* of life but a *quality* of life (2 Corinthians 2:9).

The real comfort you need at this time will come, not just from the certainty of the life you and your child will share, but from the Scriptures which tell of the fullness of that life. Most of us have absorbed the world's mentality of what heaven will be. We think of the cartoon drawings of men and women wearing halos, sitting on clouds, and strumming harps for thousands of years.

A child's existence in heaven has often been pictured as that of a chubby little cherub with a tiny set of wings. May the Holy Spirit remove that type of shallow concept and open your heart to a realistic, Bible-centered view of the realm your child has entered.

"No mere man has ever seen, heard or even imagined what wonderful things God has ready for those who love the Lord" (1 Corinthians 2:9, *TLB*). Though we cannot imagine the beauty and grandeur of the universe that will be opened to us, we do know that heaven will be a place of laughter instead of tears (Revelation 7:16, 17), of celebration and rulership (Revelation 5:9-12) and of loving fellowship. The Father has named his children "joint-heirs" with Christ Jesus, and we will "rule and reign" with him as kings and queens in creation. Instead of the idleness that some have pictured, we will be given responsibility and authority.

Your child had a great inheritance awaiting him in heaven—more than any prince of this world could dream of. In Christ's earthly ministry, he said many times that children are the greatest in the kingdom of heaven.

One young mother, a strong Christian, said, "I know what the Word says about heaven, and that my baby, Johnny, is happy and healthy with his heavenly Father. But I am sorry for the relationship of mother and son that I will have missed with Johnny." Yet many places in the Bible seem to illustrate that this life is only a "shadow" of things to come. (You may wish to read the powerful description of heaven in *The Last Battle*—the final book in the Chronicles of Narnia by C. S. Lewis.) If this life is only a "shadow" or "foretaste" of what heaven will be, then even the wonderful relationship between mother and child cannot compare to the relationships that we will enjoy in heaven.

Loretta Benfield shares how powerful the Word of God was in her life when her first-born daughter, Renee, stopped breathing after only three hours of life: "I lay in the hospital room, knowing Renee was in heaven, but thinking, 'That baby needs me! I was so ready to love her and nurse her and hug her when she cried!'

"Then I read in the Book of Revelation verses that show Jesus wiping away tears and drying eyes and making sure no one is hungry or thirsty (Revelation 7:17). Those verses are special to everyone, I guess, but when a mother applies them to her child and the care it is getting in heaven, they take on a whole new meaning."

Your season of grief will not pass quickly. But in this season, the Word of God can become much more than just a book; it can be the spiritual food that sustains you, giving you the strength to face each day.

SOME IMMEDIATE DECISIONS

Immediately following a late-pregnancy miscarriage, or stillbirth, you must decide whether or not to have a memorial service for the infant.

In some states, the law says that the hospital must make arrangements for the deceased fetus weighing over 500 mg., but that arrangements for any fetus or infant over this weight become the responsibility of the parents. You then must decide whether to have a memorial service, a funeral, or no service. Your clergyman and physician can offer wise counsel to help you through all of the details surrounding your decision.

In many situations, parents of a stillborn have been advised by friends and relatives to have no service. It has been thought that perhaps this would help the grieving mother to "get over" the trauma more quickly. But the SIDS (Sudden Infant Death Support) organization, which has worked with hundreds of couples nationwide, has observed that the parents work through the trauma more successfully when there *is* a memorial service.

Reports one SIDS spokeswoman from Seattle: "Too often, friends and relatives try to act as if the stillbirth never happened in an attempt to help the parents. The baby was not known to them. But the infant was very real to the mother who carried this tiny life. To most, a memorial service is important, an acknowledgment that the infant was a very real part of their family.

"The service, however, need not be expensive or even public. It is often held at graveside with the pastor and close friends and relatives. Some husbands and wives even prefer a private graveside time with only their minister present."

Another suggestion made by SIDS is that the mother have a keepsake to treasure from among the belongings that were prepared for the lost baby. "I am glad that I kept the soft yellow bunting I crocheted during my pregnancy with Jessica," Sue Miller confides when she thinks of her experience with stillbirth. "From time to time I have taken it out of the hope chest and shown it to my little boys, and we have talked about their having a little sister in heaven."

Another question asked immediately is whether the parents will consent to the dead infant being autopsied. Many initially feel like saying no, yet the information gained can be of enormous value in the planning of future healthy pregnancies. Depending on the cause of death, the parents may then choose to give birth to the next child in a hospital where there is a strong neonatal intensive care unit. The physician may even suggest that future pregnancy examinations be made at that unit.

MOVING THROUGH THE STAGES OF GRIEF

A man or a woman who walks "through the valley of the shadow of death" passes through several common stages of grief. (Feelings which follow a miscarriage were mentioned in chapter one.) It will help to know what these stages are and that they are necessary. It also helps to know that you are not the only one who has experienced these differing emotions: "Dear friends, don't be bewildered or surprised when you go through the fiery trials ahead, for this is no strange, unusual thing that is going to happen . . ." (1 Peter 4:12, *TLB*).

1. *The first stage is one of shock.* Therapists say this works as a temporary anesthesia, a brief escape from the pain of reality. It may last a few hours or a few weeks, and is good— as long as it is temporary. This is why it is beneficial for the parents to go ahead with making decisions and doing all that they can for themselves.

"My neighbors were so wonderful after the

loss of our premature twins," Brenda Soden-berg recalls. "But I asked them to please let me do my own housework—it kept me from just sitting and staring into space."

2. *You will begin to express emotions.* We must not and need not apologize for expressing our emotions. To deny them is to bottle up forces that can later do us harm. It is all right to feel angry. Your heavenly Father understands: "He knoweth your frame. . . ."

The only word of caution relates to *how* these feelings are directed. Don't direct your anger toward your mate and other loved ones, but toward the situation.

The expressing of emotion is often much harder for the father, especially if he was raised to be unexpressive, to be "tough." But the Bible shows us that strong, hearty men of faith were able to weep when going through trial. King David said that his tears were with him "all night long."

3. *You will also experience depression and feelings of loneliness.* After a strong surge of emotions or after a physical ordeal such as labor and delivery, you may feel "drained" or "wrung out."

The only way to walk through this normal stage of grief is to take one day at a time. Allow the Word of God to speak to you each day and go to the Lord for strength each day.

A promise to claim: "My grace is sufficient

for thee" (2 Corinthians 12:9, *KJV*).

4. *You may feel panicky.* Perhaps you have had thoughts such as, "I cannot stand this; I will have a nervous breakdown." Chapter six will help you to deal with emotional lies.

5. *You may feel guilty or responsible for the loss.* This was also mentioned in chapter one. Christians are so different from nonbelievers in this area, for we have available cleansing through confession and understanding through grace.

Neurotic or unreasonable guilt loses its power more quickly when an individual is able to verbally express that false guilt to a wise and trustworthy person.

6. *You may resist a return to normalcy.* Even when you are progressing through the valley of grief, there is something in you that resists returning to regular activities, to "life as before." You may feel that others are forgetting the loss you suffered, and your heart says it is wrong to let the memory of your lost child be erased. Sometimes acquaintances are overly cautious, avoiding the mention of the infant in an effort to save you further suffering.

Inner resistance is also very common, but to remain in the valley of grief—to wrap the blanket of grieving around you and become comfortable in it—does no honor to the memory of the infant you lost.

What does give infinite value to the memory

of that little one is the reaffirmation of the knowledge that "your labor was not in vain."

7. *The last stage is the return of hope and the affirmation of reality.* We do not return to our "old selves," for every significant grief experience adds something different to our lives. "Depending on the way we have responded to this event we are either stronger people than we were before, or weaker—either healthier in spirit or sicker," says Dr. Granger Westberg, founder of Wholistic Health Centers.

We must allow Jesus Christ to guide us through our grief—a grief which Dr. Westberg terms "Good Grief," or a nondestructive, good kind of grief. Then one day we will realize we once again have the courage to love, to face life with excitement, even to make plans for another child.

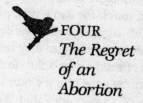

FOUR
The Regret of an Abortion

*Speak ye comfortably to Jerusalem, and cry
unto her, that her warfare is accomplished,
that her iniquity is pardoned. . . .*

*If our heart condemns us, God is greater
than our heart. . . .* Isaiah 40:2 and 1 John
3:20, KJV

In the late eighteenth and early nineteenth
centuries, doctors began a practice which they
were certain would benefit patients suffering
from a multitude of problems. It was called
"blood letting." The best, most knowledgeable
physicians of that time believed that "bad
blood" was responsible for many ailments,
from influenza to whooping cough. Thus they
would readily cut a patient's veins and "bleed"
that individual in an attempt to cure him.

In time, those doctors learned that they were

absolutely, horrifyingly wrong. Many patients were weakened, while many others actually died because of the blood-letting "cure" which they thought would be helpful.

In much the same way, physicians and many health services today readily offer women patients a treatment they believe in—*abortion*. It is offered as the solution for many situations, from the case of a woman in bad health to the case of a pregnancy that is simply unwanted.

(Interestingly, physicians who readily give abortions break the Hippocratic Oath, which they recited as they began their practice: " . . . I will give no deadly medicine to anyone nor suggest any such counsel; and in like manner I will not give to a woman a pessary to produce an abortion.")

The most recent statistics from the Center for Disease Control in Atlanta, Georgia, tell us that approximately one out of eight American women has already had at least one legal abortion. After an abortion many women suffer physically, as well as emotionally and spiritually. *Regret* is one of the most torturous, most emotionally draining of all human feelings. It can cause a woman to feel as weakened and lifeless as if she had had blood drained from her body. Regret can become a cloud over her life, causing the past to cast a shadow over both the present and the future.

Several stressful situations can lead to an

abortion—situations which leave different afterthoughts and different reasons for regret.

One of the most common reasons for regret is that many times, especially in the case of youthful unplanned pregnancies, a woman may feel that she was "pushed" or even "forced" into choosing to abort:

"I went to the free clinic at the university," a girl named Suzette recalls. "They urged me to get an abortion, and the whole procedure was over before I hardly had a chance to think about what was happening.

"My fiancé threw a fit when I told him I was going to have a baby," Bonnie remembers. "He said, 'No, you're not, not if you plan to marry me.' He was in pre-med and scared about finances. I loved him so much, what else could I do besides get an abortion? It was his choice, not mine . . . and even though Lance and I have been married for four years, I think that, in a way, I still hold it against him."

"When I was pregnant at sixteen, my parents gave me absolutely no choice other than an abortion. Mom told me that I would break my Dad's heart if I had that baby," Diane explains. "I felt like they would disown me. I wasn't sure I wanted an abortion, but they didn't give me a chance to make my own decision."

Women in these situations have to deal with more than regret. They must face feelings of *bitterness* and *unforgiveness*. Your regret can never be healed unless that inner anger is healed.

Forgiving a parent or an old boyfriend is difficult, and seemingly impossible. *But forgiveness is God's way to wholeness.* He not only tells us how to forgive, he promises the inner power that will enable us to do so.

A few abortions occur because women have been advised that their pregnancies will bring them physical harm or that the fetuses they are carrying are unhealthy. Though performed for medical reasons, these abortions are often followed by tremendous regret, because they are performed on married women who desire to have a baby. One woman who dealt with this type of regret is Mrs. Karen Chisholm:

"Our doctor informed us that because of the chance of Down's syndrome, I should undergo an amniocentesis. I had that test in the sixteenth week of my pregnancy, and it indicated that the fetus I was carrying was not normal. My husband and I were fearful of raising a child with that type of severe handicap, so I chose an abortion.

"I deeply regret having chosen that abortion because we want a child desperately. Now I have discovered that Sir Arthur Liley, who invented amniocentesis, is strongly pro-life and designed this test to be used late in pregnancy if there is a risk of the Rhesus-incompatibility disease so that a fetus can be treated and *saved*. And I found a survey by Dr. Murray Feingold, an expert on birth defects, who said that the more educated parents are on the risks and limitations of amniocentesis, the more likely they are to reject the procedure. There have been laboratory mistakes even in determining the correct sex of a baby!

"I guess most of all I regret that I didn't have more faith and ask the Lord to heal that baby inside of me. And I worry about what the Lord must think of me. . . ."

A great many women regret the emotional scars they received during an abortion, scars like those talked about by a coed named Lynda from Washington State:

"When I was in high school my mom's unmarried brother came to live with us, and one night when we were home alone he forced me into bed with him and threatened to kill me if I even told. Well, I got pregnant. I had also had sex with my boyfriend close to that time, and I didn't know whose baby it was. But I'd heard about the chance of birth defects from incest and so abortion seemed the easy way out.

"Only it wasn't easy. They didn't tell me how hard the labor would be. . . .

"I feel like something awful happened in my heart when my uncle forced me, but the abortion only seemed to make the hurting worse. Now I have awful nightmares that make me go through that fear and pain of the abortion over and over again.

"And I have heard that not many girls actually get pregnant after a rape so the baby might even have been my boyfriend's.

"I'm so sorry that whole segment in my life ever happened, and I wonder if I will ever feel the same again."

One of the greatest reasons for regret comes when a woman becomes a Christian and begins to comprehend the value of every individual life, understanding that an unborn child is an eternal soul. The feeling expressed by a woman from Portland, Oregon, is common to many women from many churches:

"The fact that I had three abortions before I became a Christian still really upsets me. I guess I feel like a second-class Christian or something. The thought of seeing those beings in heaven that I sent into eternity really bothers me. And I don't feel like I can talk to any of my Christian friends about how *guilty* I still feel."

Guilt. It is so closely tied to the regret of an abortion. According to a support group called Women Exploited by Abortion, "Many women have discovered following their abortions that they are plagued by nightmares; preoccupied by the baby's perceived would-be birthdate or its age; a need to become pregnant with another baby—an 'atonement' baby. Many undertake self-destructive behavior ranging from drug or alcohol abuse to anorexia to suicide attempts."

As human beings, we can push guilt feelings down into our subconscious and try to ignore them or cover them over. But your body and your mind cannot carry the weight called "guilt." Medical studies tell us that hundreds of mental and physical illnesses are brought on by guilt. In his book *None of These Diseases,* Dr. S. I. McMillen lists everything from headaches to high blood pressure, from allergies to obesity.

Society simply tells you, "There's no need to feel guilty." The Word of God, however, hits the problem from an entirely different angle. The Bible stresses *the fullness of God's forgiveness.*

Just how "full" is God's forgiveness?

Does he offer only enough forgiveness to get you into heaven, or does he extend such an abundance of grace that you can live free from the weight of all guilt?

No matter how much you may value God's forgiveness, you have probably far under-estimated its effects. Only a handful of believers ever learn to live in the joy of truly under-standing what the heavenly Father means when he says, "My child, you are forgiven."

The Lord Jesus did not die on the cross to offer you a simple "whitewash" job on the outside, but rather to offer the power which reaches to the depths of your inner being. Scripture tells us that not only is your past forgiven, it is forgotten! "For I will be merciful to their unrighteousness, and their sins . . . will I remember no more," says Hebrews 8:12 *(KJV)*.

Then, after he forgives you, he enables you to *forgive yourself*, breaking the chains to your past and enabling you to move on. As 1 John 3:20 tells us, if our hearts condemn us, God is greater than our hearts! He does not offer simply a whitewash for your conscience—but a total *cleansing:* " . . . though your sins be as scarlet, they shall be as white as snow" (Isaiah 1:18, *KJV*).

The Lord desires to cleanse your heart and mind of all of the old heartaches, nightmares, and harmful memories. Then he will give his divine peace as a sentinel, guarding your heart and mind from any horrors of the past.

You are a three-part creation—body, soul, and spirit. The power of God is available to heal your body (if you have suffered any after-effects from the abortion), to heal your spirit, and to heal the hurts of your soul.

Dennis and Rita Bennett, well-known authors and Spirit-filled teachers, term this healing of the soul "inner healing." They encourage counselees to simply picture a past event which left them hurt, and then to picture Jesus Christ at their side during that event. One Christian man who came to them said that he had no desire to have children and that he thought it had something to do with the fact that he had forced his wife to get an abortion during her first pregnancy.

"Go back and picture that event," Dennis told him. "Where do you see yourself?"

"In the waiting room of the doctor's office, while my wife is inside having the abortion."

"Now, picture Jesus in that room with you. What do you see him doing?"

"I see him weeping," the man replied. "He is grieving over the situation, but. . . ." The tall young man began to cry. "He is looking at me with sadness, but not with anger or condemnation."

"Is there anything else?" Dennis asked softly.

"Yes," the man sobbed. "I'm going to have Jesus tell that little being that I'm sorry, that I didn't realize at the time what I was doing. Oh!" he choked as the memory became more vivid. "Baby, forgive me!"

A year later, Dennis and Rita met with the man once more. He and his wife shared the story of what a wonderful change had happened in their lives since they had learned to apply the forgiveness of the Lord to specific situations, such as the memory of the abortion. "We were Christians before," they said, "but now we know that if the Son sets you free, you will indeed be free" (John 8:36, *TLB*).

The regret of an abortion is awesome, because each infant conceived is a being of eternal destiny (see chapter two). Ephesians 2:7 is a verse that could have been penned especially for your situation, for it reminds us that "in the ages to come" God will show "the exceeding riches of his grace in his kindness toward us . . ." *(KJV)*.

Only in the ages to come will the full impact of God's forgiveness be realized, for as a believer, you will still get to share eternity with any children who were lost to you in the past.

As you are healed of the regret of an abortion, you will now be able to minister to literally hundreds of women around you who have experienced that same regret. Great ministries flow from great healings. With compassion and understanding you will answer the call of Isaiah 40:2: "Speak ye comfortably

... and cry unto her, that her warfare [her struggle] is accomplished, that her iniquity [sin] is pardoned . . ." *(KJV)*.

ANOTHER LOOK

Freedom from the Oppressor: A Case History
The following is an open letter from a twenty-eight-year-old Christian woman:

I was shocked at what began to happen to me in the past year while I was at home caring for my three- and four-year-old daughters. I am a believer, and I love my little girls very much, but on the days when they would be giving me a hard time and I would be at the end of my rope, I would find myself losing my temper and wanting to harm them. Several times I really got out of control and spanked them much harder than I meant to. It seemed like I was hearing voices in my head that told me to hurt them.

One day when I was especially angry with the children, a voice said, "Lydia, you'd be better off if they were dead." That thought came to me so strongly, and I became so terrified of actually harming them, that I just collapsed on my living room floor, crying hysterically and asking God to help me.

For a few days, I felt as if I were losing my mind. There was no one that I could talk to about these voices that had told me to hurt my kids. I just kept praying and asking the Lord to show me what was going on.

I felt that the Lord reminded me of what I had gone through in college. I had twice gotten pregnant and as a result I had two abortions, the first when I was quite far along. I was not a Christian then, but I think I still thought of each fetus as a real person, a person whose life I had chosen to end. Somehow I had just pushed those thoughts to the back of my mind and had gone on with my plans for a career.

I just didn't know how deeply guilt affects us. I got married to a wonderful man, and was able to have two beautiful, healthy daughters. Now I was being tempted to harm them! As I asked the Lord why, I realized that deep in my subconscious, I already thought of myself as a murderer. The Bible tells us not to give Satan a "foothold," and the abortions had given the devil a foothold, or a chance to get his foot in the door of my mind.

When I received Christ as my Savior, I knew he had forgiven me of my sins, but I had never specifically applied his forgiveness to the abortions. So I began to pray specifically about this guilt that for so long I had hidden, even from myself. And as I studied my Bible, the Holy Spirit led me to verses that really applied to my situation.

In 2 Corinthians 4:1, 2 *(KJV)*, I read:
" . . . As we have received mercy, we faint not; But have *renounced the hidden things . . . .*" Webster defines *renounce* as "to cast off," so I prayed a simple prayer, renouncing the abortions which had been hidden in my past.

Then in Ephesians 6:12 *(KJV)*, I read: "For we wrestle not against flesh and blood, but against . . . spiritual wickedness." I realized that the thoughts about harming the children were not my own thoughts, but that I was the target of spiritual warfare.

James 4:7 *(KJV)* told me what to do about the spiritual attack: " . . . Resist the devil, and he will flee." In the Gospels I read that Jesus had rebuked the devil and evil spirits, so in Jesus' name I rebuked the voices that had told me to physically harm my daughters.

I am so thrilled to say that I have never again been troubled with those voices. Every mother gets angry sometimes, but I am no longer unreasonable, and I am no longer out of control. And I'm finding that the Lord has released me into a new ability to express love and show tenderness to my children.

FIVE
The Child
You Placed
for Adoption

*Can a mother forget her little child and not
have love for her own son? . . . I will not forget
you. See, I have tattooed your name upon my
palm. . . . Isaiah 49:15, 16,* TLB

The pretty seventeen-year-old girl who sat
beside me in the Sunday morning service was
weeping softly. We were singing the closing
hymn of the Mother's Day service, so I took
her hand and whispered, "What's wrong,
Bobbi? Can I pray with you about something?"

"I have a hard time with Mother's Day," she
answered slowly. "Hardly anyone knows that
I am a mother."

Following the service, Bobbi and I went
to the prayer room, where she shared more
about her heartache:

"Two years ago I had a little girl and gave her up for adoption. I knew I was too young to be a good mother. Most of the time I don't feel the hurt of it, but sometimes on days like this, I worry about her. Yet there's nothing I can do for her.

"I tried to do what I thought was right for the baby and for myself. Now I wonder, *What does God think of a woman who could give away her own baby?*"

Bobbi's question did not surprise me. In my time as a social worker counseling young women with unplanned pregnancies, I have often been asked, "Does anything in the Bible apply to my situation?"

A contemporary Christian recording artist reveals the heartrending trauma of her teenage years:

"After the death of my parents, I came to the Sunset Strip in Hollywood to begin a career in rock music. But with the career came drugs and heartache and an unplanned pregnancy. I placed the baby for adoption when I was a young teenager. After that experience, I thought I'd never be able to sing a joyful song in my entire life.

"Years later, through the grace of God, I became a believer. If only I had been saved sooner, I have thought, then I could have had the inner strength to raise that baby. I wonder about the kind of home he is in, and especially if it is a Christian home. I pray continually that the little boy is being raised up knowing the Savior who is so dear to me."

Another young woman who asks to be known only as Danielle tells of feelings common to thousands of Christian women:

"My hardest battle in my spiritual walk is dealing with condemnation and guilt. Guilt because I failed as a mother. At sixteen I had a baby out of wedlock, a little boy that I named Jamie. At first I tried to keep him, but I just hadn't realized how much care babies require. By the time he was two months old, I just wasn't coping at all. The State placed him in foster care. I gave him up for adoption then because I knew that Jamie was suffering from my lack of ability as a mother.

"Now, ten years later, I have a little boy and a baby girl, and I enjoy them tremendously. But I still feel so beaten down because of failing with poor little Jamie. One day I read in the Bible that Jesus "came unto his own, and his own received him not" (John

1:11, *KJV*), and it broke my heart. I was thinking about Jamie, that he came to his own, and I was not able to receive him."

Questions. A feeling of complete helplessness. The torture of "what if" thoughts. Guilt and self-condemnation. These feelings are a weighty burden on the minds of many women who have placed children for adoption, a burden that is well concealed and seldom talked about.

Can the peace of God replace this burden?

If you are in this situation, you will be amazed at how much the Bible says about adoption. Do you know that many of Scripture's most prominent figures were given up for adoption, and yet were mightily used in God's plan for the ages?

One of the most touching examples is that of a young woman of Israel from the tribe of Levi, the natural mother of Moses. Her story is found in Exodus 2:1-10.

Placing a child for adoption is often the only choice a woman has. For the mother of baby Moses, there was no other choice, no other alternative.

The entire nation of Israel was in slavery in Egypt at that time. The children of God had been in bondage for 400 years, but in 1400 B.C., under the dominion of an evil pharaoh, their harsh treatment was intensified. This pharaoh feared the rapidly increasing number of Jews and decreed that all Jewish infant males were to be put to death.

Scripture tells us that little Moses was a beautiful child and that his mother loved him and kept him in her home for as long as she was able. When she saw that he was no longer safe in her care, she prepared a tiny basket-boat and placed it in the tall foliage at the edge of the Nile River. Miriam, the infant's sister, was left to stand guard to "see what will become of him."

It was an act of desperation, a plea which said, "God, I cannot care for this baby. I have done all I can, and now I cast him upon your mercy."

When the childless daughter of the very pharaoh of Egypt came to the river to bathe, she discovered the basket and opened it. As the baby began to weep, the Bible tells us that she "had compassion on him." This was not a normal response; the princess had been schooled in prejudice toward Hebrews and other enslaved peoples. But God sovereignly moved in her heart, and she loved little Moses as her own son.

Young Miriam was sent to "find a Hebrew nurse for the child," and of course she led the princess and Moses back to his own mother! Pharaoh's daughter even agreed to pay the Jewish woman to care for her own little boy—

the same little boy whom a short time before the woman had given up completely.

Later in the story, when Moses grew old enough to be weaned (probably several years old), the natural mother once again unselfishly gave up her claim to the child. Moses was presented to the princess, who raised him in the palace as an heir to the pharaoh of Egypt.

Can you imagine the prayerful travail of the woman's heart who new the one true God, and who wept with spiritual concern over her son? The prayers of a parent for a child are very special to the heart of God, and distance does not hinder them. In Exodus 2:24 *(KJV)* we read, " . . . And God remembered his covenant. . . ."

The call of God came upon the young man named Moses, and though given up for adoption as a child, he became supernaturally anointed to lead the entire nation of Israel out of bondage and into the "Promised Land."

Consider your situation. If you suffer spiritual condemnation, you can be totally released from that weight.

Danielle, the young mother who had felt such guilt because she had given up two-month-old Jamie, was greatly comforted when she and I read together the story of the wise and inspiring Jochebed.

"I feel that the mother of Moses and I have a lot in common. The babies all around her were being put to death by the sword. Most of the babies of the young girls around me were being put to death . . . by abortion. I kept Jamie for as long as I could, just as that biblical woman kept Moses. Then we gave them up. She was in touch with Moses for a while because she got to nurse him, and I was in touch with Jamie while he was in foster care. Then Moses went to the palace of the pharaoh, and became a mighty prince of Egypt. I do not know where Jamie went, or what he was renamed. But I am praying that it is a wonderful home—a 'palace' in a sense—and that God has a powerful plan for Jamie just like he had for Moses."

If you have wondered, *What does God think of a woman who would give up a baby?*, turn to Exodus 2 and read the story of Moses. Natural mothers who place children for adoption usually do so because *they are thinking of the welfare of the child, placing the baby's needs ahead of their own feelings*. Our heavenly Father is pleased when we make choices according to the biblical description of love: "Love is . . . never haughty or selfish or rude. Love does not demand its own way" (1 Corinthians 13:5, *TLB*).

Still another moving example of a godly woman who unselfishly gave up a much-loved child is found in 1 Samuel 1. The woman was

Hannah; her husband was Elkanah. Hannah presented her young son to the Lord, and as was sometimes done in those days, Samuel was housed in the temple in Jerusalem and "adopted" by the high priest, Eli.

Verse 28 tells us how Hannah had the emotional courage to do this. She said: "I am giving him to the Lord for as long as he lives" *(TLB)*.

It is interesting to note that in this case, the "adopting father" was not the most godly of adoptive parents. At least we know that Eli's two natural sons, Hophni and Phinehas, grew up to be very wicked men. Still, God honored Hannah's prayer, and the Lord completely overrode any poor example which may have been set for Samuel.

In 1 Samuel 2:26 *(KJV)* we read that "Samuel grew on, and was in favor both with the Lord, and also with men." In chapter three, we discover that God spoke audibly to the young lad. First Samuel 3:1 shows us the uniqueness of this calling, for it says: "The word of the Lord was precious [rare] in those days, and there was no open vision" *(KJV)*.

Samuel, the little boy loved and yet released by his natural mother, became the high priest of all Israel. He served as judge for the nation and led in overthrowing the tyranny of the Philistines. He anointed the first Jewish king named Saul and became the trusted counselor of the mighty King David.

You may have felt that any impact on the future of the child you placed for adoption is hopeless, that "all I can do is pray." We say those words, not realizing that prayer, when energized by God-given faith, is the most powerful force in the universe.

First of all, have you prayed a definite dedication prayer, committing the child you bore unto the Lord and into his protection? Second Timothy 1:12 is a promise which specifically applies to your situation: "I am sure that he is able to safely guard all that I have given him until the day of his return" *(TLB).*

Jesus has given us tremendous authority as we pray in his name. He said, "Whatever you bind on earth will be bound in heaven, and whatever you loose on earth will be loosed in heaven" (Matthew 16:19, *New International Version).* In other words, as you *bind* anything that would harm the life and growth of the child, your Father in heaven says, "So be it." And as you pray a prayer releasing mental health and happiness and salvation to that child, the Father says, "Yes. So be it."

Intercessory prayer is not bound by distance, or by how much you know of a situation. You must not have an "all-I-can-do-is-pray" attitude, for prayer is everything.

You have known the agony of surrender, of giving up something very precious. You did it for the sake of the child. Because of this very difficult act of "death to self," you can experience the presence of Jesus in a very special way. He taught us that if we selfishly try to hang on to life, we lose it, but if we give up our grasping for life, we will find what life is all about (see Luke 9:24, 25; 17:33; John 12:24, 25).

Jesus is the One who can heal your inner scars: "The Spirit of the Lord is upon me, because . . . he hath sent me to heal the brokenhearted . . ." (Luke 4:18, *KJV*).

He is the One who can "make up for lost time" and redeem the years and events which happened in your rebellion:

"I will restore to you the years [the lost time] that the locust hath eaten" (Joel 2:25, *KJV*).

"Once again you will have all the food you want. Praise the Lord, who does these miracles for you . . ." (Joel 2:26, *KJV*).

" . . . Can a mother forget her little child and not have love for her own son? Yet even if that should be, I will not forget you. See, I have tattoed your name upon my palm and ever before me is a picture of Jerusalem's walls in ruins" (Isaiah 49:15, 16, *TLB*).

"I will never, never fail you nor forsake you" (Hebrews 13:5, *TLB*).

SIX
*Freed
from the Fear
of the Future*

*For God hath not given us the spirit of fear;
but of power, and of love, and of a sound
mind.*

What time I am afraid, I will trust in thee.
2 Timothy 1:7 and Psalm 56:3, KJV

The true trauma of a miscarriage or a stillbirth
is that it can encircle a woman with a dark
cloud of fear that carries over into future
pregnancies. Some balk at the thought of a new
conception and may say, "I cannot face the
possibility of this happening again." Other
women immediately choose to try again, but
are bombarded with doubts and fears which
invade their minds and bring about a nine-
month marathon of emotional torture.

A certain amount of fear, concern, and

caution is normal, even helpful. Fear is a mechanism God has given our bodies so that, when we are confronted with danger, we take action which leads to our safety. As you face a new pregnancy, reasonable concern will give you and your husband great wisdom in dealing with your particular situation. It is wise at this time to wholeheartedly seek God's protection and the very best medical advice available.

Scripture reminds us: "In the multitude of counsellors there is safety" (Proverbs 11:14, *KJV*).

Finding the right obstetrician is always important but even more so after a miscarriage. Find someone thoroughly acquainted with recent research on the causes of miscarriage, such as mycoplasmas and other bacteria, and equipped to deal with any afflictions which may complicate a pregnancy, such as toxemia and diabetes. It is wise to seek a doctor who has had experience helping women who have delivered full-term, but stillborn infants. Having an obstetrician with access to fetal monitoring devices and with expertise in delivering babies by caesarean section is advisable.

Many women choose to remain with their previous doctor. According to the *American Journal of Medicine,* the single most important consideration for a concerned mother-to-be is that the expert be willing to be personally responsible for her care. One woman shared this: "I needed a doctor who understood my situation, one that I felt comfortable with so that I could ask questions, one who did not schedule my appointments with one of his associates."

It is important to try to see the chosen obstetrician before you conceive another child. Most specialists recommend that a woman wait at least three months after a delivery or miscarriage before attempting to become pregnant. Various anatomical abnormalities which may cause spontaneous abortion are often surgically correctible. And if you suffered a second-trimester miscarriage because of a problematic cervix, your doctor will plan procedures to strengthen the cervix in the last months of pregnancy.

Once a new pregnancy begins, discipline yourself to do all of the things which you know to be important for the health of a fetus— proper nutrition, proper rest, controlled weight gain so that you do not run the risk of toxemia, and avoidance of any harmful substances are important to any expectant mother.

If spotting occurs during a pregnancy, notify your doctor immediately. Many physicians will recommend bed rest and the avoidance of sexual intercourse for a time. Elliott McCleary, in his book *New Miracles of Childbirth* (McKay Company, 1974), notes that if the bleeding is caused by the placenta's growth inside the uterus, bed rest is prescribed "to give the placenta the best chance of reattaching itself securely to the uterine lining." Yet even in the instance of spotting or cramping, you must not let fear engulf you. Statistics show that as many as one-half of all women bleed or spot sometime during pregnancy.

Women who have lost a child due to premature birth may wish to make plans to deliver their next infant in a hospital where there is a Newborn Intensive Care Unit (NICU). These hospitals provide a type of care which was unavailable up until a few years ago, but is provided today in about 200 hospitals across the country. These centers are especially equipped to deal with RDS (respiratory distress syndrome), which accounts for about half of all premature infant deaths, as well as many other complications of delivery.

The most demanding area of your new pregnancy will not be physical, but emotional and spiritual. As we discussed earlier, some apprehension is normal, but what if your fear turns into a giant which torments you? What is the source of tormenting fear?

Psychologists tell us that at the root of unhealthy, tormenting fear is usually an exaggerated or over-stressed thought, or an inaccurate mental picture of the future. Studies have shown that at least 85 percent of the things we fear never materialize. These tormenting thoughts are termed "delusions." The Bible gives them an even simpler name—lies.

In 1 Peter 5:8 we see that, as God's children, we are the object of a powerful spiritual warfare. Jesus talked about the devil, your spiritual Enemy, in John 8:44, calling him "the father of liars" *(TLB)*.

As Christians, we need to be aware that our Enemy attempts to get us to accept tormenting lies and their resulting emotion—fear. Have you ever realized that some ideas which may come to your mind are not your own? Have you ever discovered that the things you "hear" in your mind can either be accepted (if they are according to God's promises) or rejected? Thoughts such as:

"You might as well not even try; you will never carry a baby full term."

"There is something wrong with the baby you have conceived."

"This pregnancy will be too hard on you; you will have a nervous breakdown."

These thoughts, and others like them, come occasionally to *every* pregnant woman. But if your mind is bombarded with fear, the source of that fear is the father of all lies. Still, you and I are not defenseless. God provides us with both spiritual tactics and spiritual weapons for this spiritual warfare.

First of all, you will discover that you can "put on God's whole armor so that you will be able to stand safe against all strategies and tricks of Satan" (Ephesians 6:11, *TLB*). By studying the following verses, you can see that the Lord has provided a helmet of salvation to protect the battlefield of your mind, for "we are not fighting against people made of flesh and blood, but against persons without bodies —the evil rulers of an unseen world . . ." (verse 12).

Then, in 2 Corinthians 2:11, you are given these powerful instructions:

1. Cast down "imaginations" and mental "speculations."

2. Bring every thought into "captivity" and under the Lordship of Christ.

If fearful imaginings plague you or if you have nightmares about the birth of your next child, set yourself to "cast down" these thoughts from their place of influence over your emotions. You don't have to try to accomplish this victory in your own strength alone. First John 3:8 tells us that Jesus came to destroy all the works of darkness. He is the One who brings light to the darkness of our fears.

It is also helpful to know that when Paul wrote "bring every thought into *captivity*," the Greek word he used for captivity was *aichmălōśia*. *Aichmălōśia* literally means "taken captive at sword point" (from *Vine's Dictionary of New Testament Words*). You can bring every distressing thought to sword point! What a beautiful word-picture of bringing tormenting thoughts to their knees by our use of the quick and powerful two-edged sword— the Word of God (see Hebrews 4:12).

This scriptural pattern for mental health will help you not only in this pregnancy, but for the rest of your life. Soon the infant you deliver will grow into a toddler who faces the threat of contagious diseases, into a child who faces playground cuts and bruises, and then into a teenager who faces the strain of dating years and independence. At every point in your child's life you can be beset by fear. Sooner or later, you must learn to become a mother whose confidence comes from the Lord. By his grace, you can learn *now.*

A FEAR OF MY CHILDREN'S FUTURE
Perhaps your fears do not center on the actual birth of the child, but rather on the raising of that one you will love so dearly. Today's married couples are continually bombarded with despair and fear about the future of mankind. Christians are not immune to this fear. Perhaps you have had the same feelings that were expressed by Carol:

"Everywhere I turn, I hear about the possibility of World War III, of mass starvation, of increasing crime. I have even been wondering lately if the Church will go through 'the Great Tribulation.' It makes me wonder about the wisdom of bringing children into such a troubled world. Is there a Scripture portion that deals with God's will regarding having children in hard times?"

Scriptural principles are timeless, and the one regarding God's children and conception is set forth in Jeremiah 29. As the Lord's people faced exile and slavery in Babylon, the Holy Spirit spoke through the prophet and gave these instructions: "Build homes and plan to stay; plant vineyards. . . . Marry and have children, and then find mates for them and have many grandchildren. Multiply! Don't dwindle away!" (Jeremiah 29:56, *TLB*).

Then, in verse 11, God gives the concept of his loving will, which is reinforced in the New Testament: "For I know the plans I have for you, says the Lord. They are plans for good and not for evil, to give you a future and a hope."

In this portion of God's Word, we see clearly that God wants us to have families and that he plans to bless those families in spite of external circumstances.

Though there may be valid reasons for not having children, fear is not a valid reason for the Christian. We should not make decisions based on fear.

SARAH'S EXAMPLE

It is powerful to realize that we can choose faith instead of fear. And it is especially meaningful to realize that the Bible uses a pregnant woman, Sarah, as an example of true faith: "What is faith? It is the confident assurance that something we want is going to happen. It is the certainty that what we hope for is waiting for us, even though we cannot see it. . . . Sarah, too, had faith and because of this she was able to become a mother in spite of her old age, for she realized that God, who gave her his promise, would certainly do what he said" (Hebrews 11:1, 11, *TLB*).

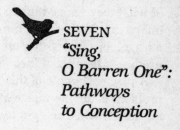

SEVEN
*"Sing,
O Barren One":
Pathways
to Conception*

*Sing, O barren, thou that didst not bear;
break forth into singing. . . .*

*He gives children to the childless wife, so
that she becomes a happy mother! Hallelujah!
Praise the Lord!* Isaiah 54:1, KJV, and Psalm
113:9, TLB

In recent years there has been a considerable
amount of teaching concerning "a healing of
your self-image." The core of this teaching is
that an individual's emotional scars, such as
those received from an overly critical parent,
can be healed by God's love. As the poor
"self-image" is healed, the individual who has
disliked himself can be transformed into an
individual at peace with himself and filled
with joy.

Unfortunately many Christians are suffering from a problem of a different "image." For them, what has fallen apart is not the inner picture of themselves, but rather the picture of what they wanted life to be. The mental image they had of their future appears to be a mirage. As a result, they are hurt and confused, needing a healing of their "life-image."

A prime example of this type of "image" problem is the life-image Marcia Taylor had for herself when she graduated from high school:

"I will go to college first, and prepare to be a teacher. I'll fall in love with a fine Christian man, and I'd like to get married when I'm about twenty-three. We'll probably work at both of our careers for a while so we can buy a home. But then I will quit work to be a homemaker. We'll have a big family—at least four children."

Marcia actually did go to college and become a teacher, and she did meet and marry a wonderful Christian man, Jeremy. But at thirty-three, her life-image was devastated. After several years of trying to conceive, Marcia was told that she would probably never have children.

After that revelation each day in the school classroom was a trial for her. Surrounded by first-graders, she was constantly reminded that she would never have a first-grader of her own. She did not quit work to stay home; her home was too empty. Yet she dreaded work, and became a harsh, impatient teacher. Soon her job was in jeopardy, and even her marriage grew shaky.

Many believers live in defeat and depression because, like Marcia, they have watched their life-image crumble.

You may find a very difficult cross to bear especially when so many women all around you terminate unwanted pregnancies through abortion. You have probably also seen many children who are uncared for or even abused. "This is *not fair!*" your heart screams.

When the cherished dream of children does not come true—or doesn't come true quickly—women react differently. Some women draw into a shell of bitterness, depression, and self-pity. Some women bury their feelings, plunging into jobs or other activities. Some, even in the twentieth century, subconsciously believe that infertility nullifies their femininity. Other women—wise women—prayerfully consider the alternatives when conception becomes a problem.

Have you been tempted to draw into a shell of self-pity and depression? You've raised the question many times: "Why do women who don't even *want* children get to have babies, and I don't?" A key factor in escaping bitterness is to remember that God does not "zap" anyone with pregnancy. Genesis 2:7 says: " . . . God formed man of the dust of the ground, and breathed into his nostrils the breath of life; and man became a living soul" *(KJV)*.

As mentioned previously, the Hebrew word translated "life" could be translated "lives." The initiation of new human lives was placed in man's dominion. God did not tell Adam, "I will multiply you." God said, "[You] be fruitful and multiply" (Genesis 1:28, *KJV*).

God established a law of human conception, just as he established all other natural laws. Because of the law of gravity, an object thrown into the air will be drawn back to the earth. Because of the law of conception, a healthy sperm brought in contact with a healthy ovum will cause fertilization and the beginning of a new human being. As a man and a woman exercise their God-given prerogative and begin a life through this natural law of conception, God breathes an eternal spirit into that life.

Each fetus conceived is not a creation of God in the "ex nihilo" or "bara" sense. *Bărá* is the Hebrew word for "creation." It is used in Genesis 1 for the creation of the universe and means "to bring into existence from nothing." A human fetus is not "ex nihilo" or "bara" because a man and a woman have supplied the sperm and the egg which give beginning substance to the tiny being.

The role of the heavenly Father in the creation of a new life is explained by understanding another Hebrew word *yatsar*. *Yatsar* is used in passages such as Isaiah 44:2: "God formed *(yatsar)* thee in the womb. . . ."

Yatsar, meaning "formed" or "created," is defined in Strong's Hebrew concordance as "to mold into shape, to fashion and frame, to imagine and then develop as a potter would 'yatsar' a vessel." Because of the heavenly Father's role in shaping the new life, each child is a divine creation. And, of course, in God's foreknowledge, there is a divine plan for every unborn child.

Yet, it is important to see that a young, unmarried girl who becomes pregnant has not been "zapped" with a pregnancy from God. Instead, she has used the prerogative God gave her to begin a new life. Neither is God punishing you by keeping you from getting pregnant; something is interfering with the natural law of conception.

For several years, *Campus Life* magazine has featured a monthly column titled "Life This Side of the Magic Kingdom." The title graphically portrays the theme of the column: we are not yet in the Magic Kingdom, or Paradise. Rather, we are in the midst of a creation flawed and complicated by the fall of man from his original state of sinless perfection.

God promised the Israelites a land flowing with milk and honey, but there were giants in the land that had to be driven out. God says in his word that "children are a heritage," but you may need to deal with some "giants" in your life before you receive your inheritance.

PATHWAYS TO CONCEPTION

The first alternative to gloom or self-pity is to *face your difficulty* head on. It is wise to seek sound medical advice, especially from experts in the fields of obstetrics and infertility. You may have specialists in your area who have a greater understanding of your particular problem than the physician you normally visit. "In the multitude of counsellors, there is safety," says Proverbs 11:14 *(KJV)*.

An amazing number of childless couples do not seek medical help for their infertility problem, or do not seek it in time. The main reason for this lack of assertiveness is fear—a fear of what really might be wrong with you. It is fear that traps an individual in the helpless state of procrastination. If you have been in this condition, grapple with your fear and seek help.

Physicians can often diagnose the cause of childlessness and recommend simple but effective treatment. Forty percent of the infertility problems in married couples lie solely with the wife. The leading causes for infertility in women are:

1. Infection. Pelvic inflammatory disease (PID) and T-mycoplasma are both caused from bacteria in the uterus, and both can go relatively unnoticed by a patient.

2. A mechanical barrier. Cervical, uterine, or tubal structure problems may prevent easy union of the egg and the sperm.

3. Endocrine disorders. Many glands in a woman's body control the menstrual cycle and ovulation. There may be a need to regulate these glands.

4. Structural defects. Malposition (in some cases called a "tipped uterus"), fibroid tumors, or other problems which may require surgical correction.

However, the first medical steps are usually taken to correct any underlying health conditions that affect a woman's reproductive cycle, such as anemia, obesity, or malnutrition.

In the husband, the most common causes of infertility are:

1. A problem in sperm production, or spermatogenesis. (A common cause of male infertility is due to a *varicocele*, a varicose vein in the testicle area. A simple operation improves sperm count in 80 percent of all cases.)

Many infections and diseases, and even stress factors, greatly impair sperm production.

2. A problem in sperm motility.

3. A blockage somewhere in the reproductive tract between where sperm are produced and where they are ejaculated.

In 20 percent of the infertility cases, the problem lies not with the male or the female, but with the couple as a unit. Often only a minor problem afflicts each partner, but together, the problems are magnified. The medical counsel which most often results in conception is in the area of coital technique. Many childless couples should not be termed "infertile," but rather "subfertile." In these couples, the chances of conceiving are lower, and therefore education about the wife's most fertile period and perhaps the use of a basal temperature chart are often very effective.

In the world around us, people often fall into the trap of "fate" or "what will be will be." Christians can be molded into this type of fatalistic thinking without realizing it, yet we think of life's events as "what has been preplanned by God." If you do not conceive quickly, do not glibly say, "Well, I guess God doesn't want there to be children in our home." Jesus taught faith that is coupled with persistence. And James 5:16 assures us that "the effectual fervent prayer of a righteous man availeth much" (KJV).

This time of waiting can be a powerful time of spiritual growth as you claim God's promises and seek God's perfect will. The Holy Spirit would say to you, "Let patience have her perfect work" (James 1:4, *KJV*).

One of the "perfect works" of patience is that, during your waiting, God has the opportunity to refine your motives. You have the opportunity to ask, "Why do we want children?" (This question is further discussed in the next chapter.) And, on the pathway to conception, you have the opportunity to grow in prayer and praise.

PRAYER AND PRAISE

For some couples, the medical prognosis may be totally negative. "I'm sorry," a sympathetic physician may have told you, "but there is nothing I can do to help you." Other couples may be told, "Medically, we can find nothing wrong. We don't know why you have not been able to conceive."

Whenever we receive a negative medical diagnosis, we are wise to follow the scriptural pattern given in James 5:14, 15 *(TLB)* for New Testament believers: "Is anyone sick? He should call for the elders of the church and they should pray over him and pour a little oil upon him, calling on the Lord to heal him. And the prayer, if offered in faith, will heal him, for the Lord will make him well; and if his sickness was caused by some sin, the Lord will forgive him."

The Bible contains the story of many miraculous healings. It is exciting to realize that one of the most common biblical healings was of couples who had not been able to bear children. Isaac, Joseph, Benjamin, Samuel, and John the Baptist—all of these mighty men of God were conceived as direct answers to prayer! The Holy Spirit may whisper to your heart that you are to be one of those who claims the promise of Psalm 113:9 *(TLB)*: "He gives children to the childless wife, so that she becomes a happy mother."

If you are trusting God for natural children, and if you have sought prayer according to the scriptural pattern and have sought medical advice, then the next step is total surrender. That may seem contradictory, but it isn't. Having told your heavenly Father of your desire to have natural children, you need to surrender that desire to him. "Gaining life by giving up life" is one of the biblical principles which is a paradox to the natural mind. But Jesus said, "Whosoever will lose his life for my sake shall find it" (Matthew 16:25, *KJV*).

An example of "surrender" would be that of a child learning how to swim. As long as the child is fearful and tense and flailing, he sinks. But as the beginner learns to relax, the water supports his weight and he learns to float.

In the area of fertility, this principle is especially important. Many physicians report that sometimes the harder a woman worries about conception, the more her reproductive cycle is interrupted. Gynecologists have often given an unusual prescription that has had amazing results: "Go on a long, relaxing vacation with your husband. Have a great time and forget about getting pregnant."

Inability to conceive, like so many conditions which plague the human body, can be triggered by mental and emotional factors. Fear, anxiety, and nervousness have been known to inhibit ovulation.

A spiritually wise woman will follow the exhortation of 1 Thessalonians 5:16, 17 *(TLB)*: "Always be joyful. Always keep on praying."

When serving on the pastoral staff of the congregation shepherded by Dr. Jack Hayford, my husband and I watched as he encouraged women who desired children to spend more time than ever before singing spiritual songs and praising the Lord. Over the years, by following this simple biblical instruction, many couples have rejoiced at the amazing results. Praise and thanksgiving restore our "inner man," and mental and emotional restoration will affect the whole body.

The effect of praise on conception is *not* mystical or farfetched, for recent reports have shown that large amounts of adrenaline in a woman's system actually act as a form of birth control. Adrenaline is the hormone that is released in our system whenever fear is present. (I encountered an amazing report about adrenaline while studying statistics on how few rape victims actually become pregnant. This is mentioned in chapter ten.)

Research is supporting what the Holy Spirit recorded in Scripture two thousand years ago, so we exhort you once again: "Worry about nothing. Pray over everything . . ."; "when Zion [God's child] travails, she brings forth children." Before physical travail, you may go through the spiritual travail of prayer.

Your difficulty in bearing children may have destroyed your preplanned "life-image." More Scripture for your situation is given in the next chapter. Your pathway to happiness and fulfillment may be different from the pathway you dreamed of taking. But one thing you can know for certain: God has a plan for your life that includes joy. Just before he went to the cross, Jesus prayed for you that you "Would be filled with [his] joy" (John 17:13, *TLB*). Remember also Job's testimony: God "knoweth the way that I take: when he hath tried me, I shall come forth as gold" (Job 23:10, *KJV*).

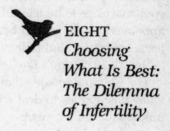

EIGHT
*Choosing
What Is Best:
The Dilemma
of Infertility*

*. . . as soon as Zion travailed, she brought
forth her children.*

*I pray that your love will keep on growing
more and more, together with true knowledge
and perfect judgment, so that you will be able
to choose what is best.* Isaiah 66:8, KJV, and
Philippians 1:9, 10, TEV

Birth is not possible without travail. The
prophet Isaiah was giving God's people a
graphic spiritual illustration when he said,
"When Zion travailed, she brought forth
children."

The Lord may lead you to "travail in prayer"
until you bring forth natural children. You may
be led to "travail" and labor through red tape
and bureaucracy until you are able to adopt

children. Or you may be anointed by the Lord to "travail" and give birth to many spiritual children.

Whatever you choose, God has planned for your marriage to be fruitful. "I chose you and appointed you to go and bear much fruit," Jesus said, "the kind of fruit that endures" (John 15:16, *Today's English Version*).

The Christian couple that faces infertility today has options to deal with that were unknown even ten years ago: test-tube babies, sperm banks, and even surrogate mothers. As a person who sees life as spiritual, and not just physiological, what do you believe? How far should you go in your efforts to bear a child?

In this difficult area, Philippians 1:9, 10 can become your daily prayer: "That we may keep on growing more and more, together with true knowledge . . . so that [we] will be able to choose what is best" *(Good News Bible).*

A WORD OF CAUTION

First, let me say simply that I am not against scientific advances or technological break-throughs. The study of fetology in recent years has enabled doctors to care for infants whose lives are in jeopardy while those babies are still in the womb. Babies with Rh incompatibility can now be saved by intrauterine blood transfusions. (With the aid of X-ray screen intensifiers and radiopague dye and special hollow needles, physicians can inject healthy blood into the circulatory system of an unborn child.) Metabolic disorders and enzyme-deficiency diseases of unborn infants are also being treated with great success.

But researchers are opening other doors, doors which may be compared to the opening of Pandora's box.

On July 25, 1978, British doctors Steptoe and Edwards gave the world the news of the first test-tube baby. To the woman with blocked fallopian tubes or a similar problem, the announcement may have seemed like heaven-sent good news.

The little girl born in England is only the beginning. Within a few short years, thousands of test-tube babies may be among us. Re-searchers are already constructing steel and glass wombs, preparing genetically to modify physical and behavioral techniques, and deep-freezing embryos for long-term storage. (In February of 1981, Prime Minister Margaret Thatcher and representatives of the British Medical Association (BMA) called a mori-torium on test-tube-baby programs, following the news that Drs. Steptoe and Edwards were planning to open a frozen embryo clinic. BMA ethics chairman Michael Thomas commented that "medical technology is running ahead of morality.")

Drs. Steptoe and Edwards became famous for the test-tube baby, but they are by no means the only scientists who have become involved in this field. As early as 1966, Dr. Pyotr Anakhin of the Academy of Medical Sciences in Moscow announced that he and a team of Soviet scientists had kept more than 250 human embryos alive in test tubes for up to six months. In 1974, Dr. Douglas Brevis stunned a British medical conference by saying that after thirty attempted embryo implantations, three had been successful. This one statement alone shouts caution to any believer in agreement with the premise of the first chapters of this book: the fact that every embryo is a human life with a soul and an eternal spirit.

One new field open to infertile couples seems less controversial than "test-tube babies"—the technique of artificial insemination. But—is it?

Artificial insemination by donor is usually accomplished by a woman's physician making contact with one of a dozen "sperm banks" across the nation. Cryogenics Laboratories in St. Paul is a national leader, and supplies physicians in over forty-five cities. The sperm used by Cryogenics are from only thirty-five "carefully chosen" donors. How many hundreds of babies being born in the U.S. have the same donor as their natural father? Shocking statistics tell us that perhaps a million Americans have already been born as the product of artificial insemination, and that this number increases at the rate of more than 20,000 a year.

In New York State, an engaged young couple was recently denied a marriage license for this very reason. The handsome man and his fianceé had been born in different states, and did not meet until college, where they fell deeply in love. But both had been products of artificial insemination by donor. A medical expert discovered that both mothers had received sperm from the same sperm bank, and further investigation showed that the sperm was from the same donor. The two lovers could not legally marry; they were half brother and sister!

Robert K. Graham is the founder of a sperm bank which limits donors to high IQ scientists and Nobel Prize winners. In May of 1982, he announced the first successful birth—a baby girl was born to a Chicago woman who had been impregnated with sperm from an eminent mathematician. "A few choice athletes may be the way to go now. They're high class animals," Graham said in San Diego's paper, the *Union*.

If many children are fathered by the same sperm bank donor, it is inevitable that some of these individuals will meet and fall in love, like the unsuspecting New York couple.

Nothing causes mental retardation as surely as the intermarriage of closely related men and women. Well-meaning scientists may bring about the exact opposite of the "high class animals" they have planned.

Even without physical considerations, the legal complications of the future may be awesome. Ted Howard and Jeremy Rifkin, in their book *Who Should Play God?*, describe a recent legal battle which raged over a child conceived by artificial insemination *with* the husband's permission. In this case, it is believed that the woman's physician had located a suitable donor. Several years after the child's birth, the couple divorced. The authors explain:

"The husband wanted visitation rights to see the child. The wife argued in court that her ex-husband had no such right because he was not the child's natural father. He countered that he had given signed permission and had provided for the child as his own. A New York court granted the man visiting rights, but then the woman and her child moved to Oklahoma. There a court reversed the New York decision on the grounds that the ex-husband was not the child's genetic father.

"This ruling raised more legal questions than it answered. Could the donor arrive in town one day and demand to see his child? If the woman could learn the donor's identity, could she sue him for child support? Could the child one day claim to be the donor's heir? Strange questions to be sure, but very real for one million Americans."

Emotional as well as physical characteristics can be genetically transferred, and if all of this were not enough, there are vast spiritual implications to consider. In this small book we cannot deal in depth with technology's aids to pregnancy, but if you or a couple you know have ever considered artificial insemination, surrogate motherhood or "in vitro" conception, please do two things: Study the subject prayerfully from such books as *Who Should Play God?* by Howard and Rifkin (Dell Publishing Company), and seek godly counsel.

In recent years in America, headlines have been made by "surrogate mothers," women willing to be impregnated by artificial insemination, who bear the child and then give it to the father, usually for a substantial sum of money. This "new" idea is being considered by couples whose infertility problem lies with the wife instead of the husband. But—is it a "new" solution for childless couples? Hardly.

Arranging for "surrogate mothers" was a common practice in the ancient world; in fact, several instances are recorded in the Old Testament. The lifelong outcome of these arrangements is recorded for all to see.

In Genesis 16:2, we read of the heartbreak

of Sarah, the childless wife of Abraham. After years of waiting for the Lord to fulfill his promise of an heir, Sarah told her husband, "Behold . . . I pray thee, go in unto my maid . . . that I may obtain children by her. And Abram hearkened to the voice of Sarai" *(KJV)*. Then, in verse 4 we read that when Hagar had conceived and borne the child Ishmael, "her mistress Sarah was despised in her eyes."

The problems that arose in the household between Ishmael and Abraham's next son, Isaac, lasted for their entire lifetime. Indeed, the problems have lasted for centuries, for Isaac became the patriarch of the Israelite nation, while Ishmael fathered the peoples of Arab extraction.

Another troubled story of surrogate mothers, Bilhah and Zilpah, is told in Genesis 29. The children of these two women were fathered by Jacob, the grandson of Abraham.

CHOOSING WHAT IS BEST

Considering all the options, how do you follow the advice of Philippians 1:9, 10: "[Grow] more and more, together with true knowledge . . . so that you will be able to choose what is best" *(Today's English Version)*. How much of the medical and scientific advances available to help with fertility should you seek? How long should you keep trying to carry full term if you have had several miscarriages? At what point should you be open to adoption, or to the other alternative: emotional and spiritual parenting?

It is extremely important that you know the promise of James 1:5: "If any of you lack wisdom, let him ask of God, that giveth to all men liberally, and upbraideth not; and it shall be given him" *(KJV)*. And Proverbs 16:9 instructs us, "We should make plans counting on God to direct us" *(TLB)*.

The pathway on which he leads you may be different from the pathway set before another couple in your exact situation. In no way can we assume that what is right for one couple is necessarily right for another, or that what is God's will for one couple is always his will for another couple. His will for your life can be discovered as you search his Word, seek him in prayer, and seek godly counsel, trying to "avoid the godless mixture of contradictory notions which are falsely called 'knowledge'" (1 Timothy 6:20, *Phillips Translation*).

In your choice, it is imperative that you and your spouse come to total agreement *as a couple.* It is in your unity, your "agreement," that spiritual power will be released in Jesus' name. Too many couples pursue a course which later brings confusion or sadness because one or both of the partners did not fully express his or her feelings and convictions. In decision-making, "Two are better than one . . . and a threefold cord [two partners joined with the Holy Spirit] is not quickly broken" (Ecclesiastes 4:9, 12, *KJV*).

One indication that a decision has been made according to the will of God is the *peace of God*. As you surrender your will to him, asking his help in "choosing what is best," the choice you make for your individual situation should be accompanied by a sense of that peace.

It is the peace of God which will guard your hearts and minds.

It is the peace of God which "passeth understanding" that will cushion you from any bumps that lie in the pathway before you.

It is the peace of God that will settle on your home like the gentle dove that rested on Christ at his baptism. As you make your decision, you can hear your Father say, "These are my beloved children, in whom I am well pleased."

 NINE
*The Spirit
of Adoption:
Adopting
and Spiritual
Parenting*

*Break forth into singing, and [shout] aloud,
thou that didst not travail with child: for more
are the children of the desolate . . . Enlarge
your house; build on additions; spread out
your home! For you will soon be bursting at
the seams!*

*For ye have all received the Spirit of
adoption, whereby we cry, Abba, Father.*
Isaiah 54:1, 2, KJV, TLB, and Romans 8:15, KJV

Your first option, if you have dreamed of a
house filled with children and have none, is to
remain unhappy. The second option, as presented in previous chapters, is to seek divine
healing and medical help. The third option is
to open your heart to the possibility of
becoming an adoptive parent, just as God has

opened his heart to receive us as his children, for " . . . we should behave like God's very own children, adopted into the bosom of his family, and calling to him, 'Father, Father' " (Romans 8:15, *TLB*).

There is a special understanding of the very nature of God in the heart of Christian men and women who choose to adopt. Throughout the Old Testament, the Father makes it clear that the orphans, the homeless, the deserted, and the defenseless are very special in his sight. James 1:27 *(TLB)* says, "The Christian who is pure and without fault, from God the Father's point of view, is the one who takes care of orphans and widows. . . ." In many Scripture passages, the Lord warns that anyone who takes advantage of a homeless child will deal with his anger. In Jeremiah 22:3 *(TLB)*, the Lord says, "Be fair-minded. Do what is right! Help those in need of justice! . . . Protect the rights of aliens and immigrants, orphans and widows; stop murdering the innocent!" The alternative to obeying God's commands is alienation from his blessings, shame, destruction, and other evidences of his anger.

The Bible also presents the life stories of adopted children who became the greatest leaders of the faith, children who from infancy were touched with special anointing. In chapter five, we mentioned Moses, but there are many others, like the Prophet Samuel and the beautiful Queen Esther, whose faith and courage saved her entire nation.

There are many reasons why you may feel hesitant about adoption. The most common reason is that many have heard, through well-meaning friends or social workers, that adoption in this day and age is extremely difficult. We'll deal with the inavailability of adoptable children later in the chapter; first, let's think about other, more subtle reasons.

Barbara E. Menning, founder of Resolve Incorporated, a support group for infertile couples, says: "It is interesting that among infertile couples, some are child-oriented and some are very pregnancy-oriented. Most express desire for both the pregnancy and the end result, the child." In her book, *Infertility: A Guide for the Childless Couple,* she identifies several reasons for wanting a pregnancy:

1. *A desire on the part of the wife to experience the bodily changes of pregnancy.* Acquaintances may have described the state of pregnancy as a "glowing" time, not the very real time of stretch marks, pressure, and heartburn that it may be. Still, it is very normal to be intensely curious about what it feels like to have a baby inside of you, swelling and growing and finally being born. There is also a current return to breast-feeding, and many desire the lactation that follows normal pregnancy.

Though there are valid reasons for desiring the state of pregnancy, it is crucial to work through the false concept that the ability to carry natural offspring would make you "more of a woman." This idea has plagued women for centuries, and even makes subtle inroads into the thinking of modern women. You may need to deal with a never-admitted feeling that pregnancy would make you more fulfilled, more feminine.

2. *A desire on the part of the husband to sire a child as proof of his masculinity.* Perhaps a husband has heard other men say that they feel proud and more virile when their mates are pregnant. Though most men today are intellectually aware that siring a child is no measure of manhood, there may still be hidden feelings which a husband must face and work through.

3. *A desire in the couple for genetic continuity.* There is a natural curiosity about what a couple's combined genetic factors would produce. And it is normal to desire children "in your own image," or to have a baby which would look like "a chip off the old block." Some couples avoid considering adoption because they worry about finding a child that would "fit" into their home. Yet through honest thinking and earnest prayer, many couples have realized that factors other

than exact physical resemblance can make a child their own.

Many couples, however, are not as desirous of pregnancy as they are of the end result—a child. These couples would openly consider adoption, except for two major obstacles.

First of all, for many people there is a natural *fear of the unknown.* Until you begin to look into the different methods of adoption, the entire process may seem so complicated, so tied up with red tape, that you fear adopting because it seems beyond comprehension. You are afraid because you've heard that it is expensive to the point of being prohibitive or that you would have no choice in the children that are placed in your home. As you learn about adopting, the fear of this "unknown" process and of "unknown children" will lessen. (Besides the informal advice given in this chapter, chapter ten includes a list of many adoption placement agencies.)

Second, modern couples realize that it is more difficult to adopt children than it was in the past.

Until the 1970s, adopting a child of one's own race was a relatively easy option for infertile men and women. But the accessibility of abortions, the availability of birth control, and the number of unwed mothers who choose to keep their infants (70 percent) have greatly reduced the number of available babies in the U.S.

(It is ironic that while infants are in very short supply, there are other children who must wait to have their "own homes." These include children of school age, siblings of two or more children, children with medical handicaps or learning problems, and children of mixed backgrounds. Some "handicaps" are no more than partial hearing loss or learning problems which can be corrected by love, but until you meet one of these "special children" you may fear the label on their file.)

Another source of young, healthy children has been infants and preschoolers from other countries. Every year, war and tragedy around the globe leave a great number of orphaned or deserted children.

Though many may have been discouraged by statistics, by agencies, or by a friend's experiences with adoption difficulties, people who are persistent in their search can find children to adopt. You can rejoice, for "he who seeks [persistently goes after] will find" (Matthew 7:7, *Amplified*).

If unbelieving couples are rewarded for their diligence, how much more confident should be the Christian husband and wife who cover the adoption process with the power of prayer! The road to finding the child, or the children who are perfect for your home may seem difficult.

But you can receive much encouragement from the exhortation given in Galatians 6:9 *(TLB)*: "And let us not get tired of doing what is right, for after a while we will reap a harvest of blessing if we don't get discouraged and give up."

AGENCY ADOPTION

The primary means of adoption is through state-licensed agencies (in five states this is the *only* means of adoption). There are some advantages to agency adoption:

1. Agencies usually have the largest number of available children.

2. You can be sure that the child placed through an agency has had thorough medical screening so that any medical problems are known.

3. You can know that the child you receive has been fully relinquished before being placed in your custody.

4. Your identity will be kept totally anonymous.

It is important to know, however, that agencies do sometimes label good, happily married couples as "unacceptable." Age and financial status are two of those reasons. Another major reason is if a couple is considered "inflexible."

Flexibility is the greatest characteristic

agencies seek in adoptive parents. According to Cynthia Martin, in her book *Beating The Adoption Game,* "The couple that firmly states they want a Caucasian infant under four months old with no physical defects is in trouble." The couple that says, "We prefer an infant, but we are open to other possibilities," is far more likely to get on the list. And, if you do not get on the list, you have no chance of adopting through that agency.

Remember, after you are on the list and your home study is completed, you have the option of turning down any child about whom you are contacted. If you are notified about a child who has some problem you do not feel capable of handling—such as a medical problem requiring considerable financial support—you will have the option of giving a negative response without being taken off the list.

You should also know that, if you are rejected by an agency, you can fight that rejection (see suggested reading material on page 130).

PRIVATE ADOPTION

The next category of adoption is *private adoption,* or *independent adoption.* This means that an available child is made known to you through a private party, such as your lawyer, your doctor, or your pastor. You usually pay the biological mother's maternity fee and all legal costs through a lawyer that you hire. In many states, you will also need to complete a home study to qualify. The success and safety of a private adoption rests primarily on one thing—the quality of the lawyer who represents you. He should be well experienced in handling the legal points of adoption, and if possible, be a personal acquaintance.

(A private adoption, is *not* a black-market adoption. "Black-market babies" are those for whom a large sum of money is exchanged—sometimes as much as $20,000 or $30,000.)

One couple who successfully adopted a lovely daughter through private contacts wholeheartedly recommends their method—the use of a resumé. A good, clear, and accurate resumé is vitally important. In addition to identifying the couple, their address, and telephone number, the resumé should relate the couple's interest and desire to adopt a baby. Background information—hometowns, education, schools, professional/work experience, hobbies, even church affiliation—can all be given. The point is that the "birth mother" must be given as full a picture as possible of the people who are interested in adopting her baby.

The next step is typing up the information, making photocopies, and sending them to friends, relatives, and professional people such as lawyers, obstetricians, and ministers in one's denomination. As with a couple who recently adopted a baby using this method, patience is the key word. The author Barbara J. Berg recounts her own experience with the resumé in her excellent article "Our Fail-safe Way to Adopt" (*Parents Magazine*, February 1983). Her "waiting period" was less than three months!

NOTE: For a practical, though brief, review of laws on private adoption, Lori B. Andrews' article "Laws on Private Adoption" is a good place to start. Her article appeared in the February 1983 issue of *Parents Magazine*.

As you begin to search for a child, how do you know which door to knock on, which way to begin? Parents who have been successful in adopting will advise you to pursue more than one direction at a time. Pray for wisdom and even for divine inspiration.

We should make plans, counting on God to direct us. Commit your work to the Lord, and then it will succeed (Proverbs 16:3, 9, *TLB*).

In your time of waiting to conceive a child or of waiting to adopt, you have a chance to do something that parents who easily conceive may never do. You have an opportunity for the Lord to refine your motives in wanting to have a child. Some couples become parents because of pressure from family and society. Perhaps

all of their friends have children and they
begin a family to "fit in."

Some hope that children will strengthen a
marriage.

Some think that children will give them a
chance to relive their own childhood.

Others think that being a parent will bring
fulfillment.

You have an opportunity for God to prepare
your heart to love and care for a child for the
child's sake, not for anything that child may
give you in return. You have an opportunity
to be spiritually prepared for parenting and for
all of the challenge it involves. Instead of being
anxious and worried, thank God for this season
of waiting. Used as a time of preparation, it
can become a great blessing.

WHEN YOU ADOPT A CHILD

Just as physical weakness in the form of
allergies can be passed down through parents,
so can spiritual weaknesses such as rebellion
or anger. When parents are deeply involved in
sin, it sets in motion a chain reaction that can
reach to subsequent generations (see Exodus
20:5). But God shows mercy to thousands who
turn from their sin by loving him (Exodus
20:6), and any child can break the spiritual
chain of the past and begin a new chain of
God's blessings (Deuteronomy 12:28).

The Word of God shows us clearly that "all have sinned and come short of the glory of God," not just the parents of the child you are adopting. But Christian parents are finding the wisdom of following the biblical example of presenting the child to the Lord and praying a powerful prayer of dedication.

Present the child to the heavenly Father, and ask for his help and supernatural wisdom in bringing up the little one. Ask him to free the child from any spiritual heritage which would lead to bondage and from any spirit of rejection. Pray in the name and through the blood of our Lord Jesus Christ, and release the child to the freedom and potential of a life under Christ's lordship. "For the power of the life-giving Spirit—and this power is mine through Christ Jesus—has freed me from the vicious circle of sin and death" (Romans 8:2, TLB).

Bill Gothard, founder of Basic Youth Conflicts seminars, has done extensive study on the emotional conflicts which adopted children can encounter. Though one may not agree with all of the conclusions he draws from his research, he gives several suggestions which are very helpful to adopting couples:

1. Hold your adopted children "in an open hand" seeing that every child is only entrusted to the parents by the Lord. Love is not possessive or jealous (1 Corinthians 13).

2. Often adoptive parents may try to live as though the natural parent did not exist, but this often creates more questions in the mind of a child. As adopted children grow older, do not fear or reject their curiosity about the natural parents.

Even more important, be able to tell the child you adopted how God specifically led in his or her coming to your family, how God opened doors as answers to prayer. The child needs the reassurance of God's loving leading in his life. Build the child's self-worth by assuring him that he has been specially chosen and that God has a very wonderful plan for his life. Encourage the adopted child to focus on his heavenly Father, who must be the emotional security for us all.

SHOULD YOU CONSIDER FOSTER PARENTING?

The Foster Parents program in our nation is a necessary organization for providing temporary care for minors whose parents are, for any number of reasons, unable to care for them. It is the word *temporary* that should cause hesitation on the part of couples who have never before been parents.

In the system as it exists today, foster children in your care may be returned to the care of the natural parents at any time. Foster parents often comment on the heartache they feel when children are removed from their home just when they felt they were making progress in the emotional health of those children. For the first-time parent, the foster care system has restrictions (such as the amount of discipline you may administer) which would make your experience so painful that you might wrongly judge your ability to cope with children.

However, besides applying as foster parents with the state in which you live, you may also apply to serve as a foster parent to adoption agencies. The guidelines of the agencies and the amount of time a child may remain in your home differ from the practices of government foster care programs. In fact, couples who serve as foster parents with adoption agencies may find that it shortens the time they wait to adopt permanently.

SPIRITUAL PARENTING

Whether or not you conceive children or legally adopt, there is yet another type of parenting which is very real and extremely important, yet many Christians totally overlook it: spiritual parenting.

The Apostle Paul is a father of the faith to us all, but he had several spiritual sons into whom he poured his life and ministry. One such young man was Timothy, the recipient of two of the epistles. The story of Timothy's conversion and relationship with Paul can easily be pieced together from Acts 14:6-23, 16:1, and 2 Timothy 1:5. In 1 Timothy 1:2, Paul wrote, "Unto Timothy, my own *son in the faith . . ." (KJV,* italics mine).

Young Timothy was devoted to Paul, and so it was arranged that he accompany the apostle on the missionary tours. Later, Paul left Timothy in charge of the churches in Asia Minor. Timothy became an able pastor and overseer because of Paul's influence on his life. In one instance, Paul wrote, "Thou hast fully known my doctrine, manner of life, purpose, [and] faith" (2 Timothy 3:10, *KJV).* The life and the character of the Apostle Paul were reproduced in Timothy in such a way that he was probably molded in Paul's image more than he would have been as a natural son.

The words of Isaiah 49:20-22 hold special meaning in this regard: "The generations born in exile shall return and say, 'We need more room! It's crowded here!' Then you will think to yourself, 'Who has given me all these? For most of my children were killed and the rest were carried away into exile, leaving me here alone. Who bore these? Who raised them for me?'

"The Lord God says, 'See, I will give a signal to the Gentiles and they shall carry your little sons back to you in their arms, and your daughters on their shoulders' " *(TLB).*

Spiritual parenting, like natural parenting, happens over years of time and takes much effort and much prayer. But the rewards cannot be put into words; and the results are eternal. When God allows you to have "children in the faith," those children will go on to reproduce other spiritual children! And we will say, like Paul said to Timothy, "Henceforth there is laid up for me a crown of righteousness, which the Lord, the righteous judge, shall give me at that day" (2 Timothy 4:8, *KJV).*

TEN
*"Comfort Ye,
My People"*

*Comfort, oh, comfort my people, says your
God. Speak tenderly to Jerusalem and tell her
that her sad days are gone. Her sins are
pardoned, and the Lord will give her twice as
many blessings. . . .*

   *The Spirit of the Lord is upon me, because
he hath anointed me to preach the gospel to
the poor; he hath sent me to heal the brokenhearted. . . .* Isaiah 40:2, TLB, and Luke 4:18, KJV

Great ministry flows from people who have
had great healings. Notice I did not say, "Great
ministry flows from people who have gone
through great hurts." It is possible to go
through tragedy and trouble, and not allow
God to heal your inner scars. But the woman
or the man who has received emotional healing

becomes a channel so that divine healing may flow to others.

The Lord has a way of taking the circumstances in life which could have destroyed us and turning those things around so that they become powerful tools of ministry. If, after the emotional pain discussed in this book, you have grown closer to your heavenly Father and stronger in faith, you can say with King David in Psalm 57:6 *(TLB):* "My enemies have set a trap for me . . . But look! They themselves have fallen into it!"

The emotional battle you endured and the victory you are winning can place the hope of victory in the heart of many others.

In Isaiah 51:3, God promises to "comfort all [the] waste places" *(KJV).* And again, in Isaiah 61:4 he promises to "raise up the former desolations" *(KJV).* The months of your life which may have seemed fruitless or "wasted" because a pregnancy did not bring a child to your home can be fruitful in a different way. Do you see, like the Apostle Paul, that all that has happened to you can bring about the furtherance of the gospel?

The feeling which so often keeps believers from reaching out in ministry is *a sense of inadequacy.* This is why portions of this chapter deal with his promises to fill and use you. You may never feel "spiritual" enough to become a ministering person. Still, the experience you have been through has given you "God's words of wisdom." As the Apostle Paul explained it: "So that I may know what I may say to all these weary ones."

The circumstance which often keeps believers from being effective channels of ministry is a lack of *information.* Be a diligent and faithful steward in the area in which you reach out to comfort others. Hosea 4:6 tells us, "My people are destroyed for lack of knowledge" *(KJV).* (This verse is profoundly significant in the area of abortion—lives are perishing because Christians are not supplying information and godly knowledge.)

The heart attitude which renders many sincere Christians ineffective is *forgetting the value of one.* We live in a day of mass media, mass production, and even mass evangelism. We read about a brother or a sister in Christ who is touching thousands of lives on the mission field and we think, "Now *that's* ministry!"

Maybe you have forgotten the infinite importance of reaching *one* life.

You may never be head of an adoption board or lead a pro-life rally or speak to a convention about "problem pregnancies." But if you are willing to reach out to touch just one individual who is hurting so that he or she is changed by the life of Jesus, then your ministry has more value than can be measured, for that one life has more eternal value than can be measured.

In Luke 15, Jesus emphatically teaches the value of one. Three parables shout the message that, to God, the individual is priceless: the parable of the woman who lost a wedding keepsake-coin, the parable of the shepherd who left ninety-nine sheep and went seeking the one, and the parable of the prodigal son. In several instances in the Book of John, Jesus drew away from the multitude for intimate conversation with an individual. God treasures each human being so greatly that he "numbers the very hairs of your head"!

Reaching out in Jesus' name becomes easy as you see the individual through his eyes and comprehend the value of one person. . . .

The value of that one young woman you know in your church who just had a miscarriage. . . .

The value of the neighbor who told you that she had an abortion last year, and that it still bothers her. . . .

The infinite value of that one unborn child being carried by the teenager who lives down the road and has no one to turn to. . . .

WHEN YOU FEEL INADEQUATE
"I am glad to be a living demonstration of Christ's power, instead of showing off my own

power and abilities," (2 Corinthians 12:9, *TLB*). He promises anointing (divine ability): "But the anointing which ye have received of him abideth in you, and ye need not that any man teach you . . ." (1 John 2:27, *KJV*).

He promises wisdom: "If you want to know what God wants you to do, ask him, and he will gladly tell you, for he is always ready to give a bountiful supply of wisdom to all who ask him; he will not resent it" (James 1:5, *TLB*).

Your training in counseling may be lacking, but the Apostle Paul combined all effective counseling principles when he said simply,

"Bear one another's burdens," and
"Weep with those who weep."

WHEN YOU NEED FURTHER INFORMATION
1. *For ministry to women who have experienced miscarriage or death of an infant:* You may contact your local office of SIDS (Sudden Infant Death Syndrome Foundation) for printed material. If there is no local chapter, you may consider starting one, or a support group which is similar. You can write for information at the national office:

Sudden Infant Death Syndrome Foundation
2 Metro Plaza, Suite 205
8240 Professional Place
Landover, Michigan 20785

Some Do's

DO be available—to run errands, to help with the other children, or whatever seems needed.

DO talk sincerely about the situation, saying you are sorry about what happened to the baby and about their pain.

DO talk about the uniqueness of that child.

Do listen; allow them to talk openly and to express whatever stage of grief they are in at the time.

DO give special attention to brothers and sisters, who also hurt and are in need of comfort that their parents may not be able to give them for a while.

DO assure the parents that they did everything they could, that the medical care offered was the best available, or whatever else you know to be true and positive so that a false sense of blame is minimized.

DO allow them to enter the routine of daily life as much as they are able to.

DO share the comfort gained.

Some Don'ts

DON't avoid them because you are uncomfortable or feel anxious about what to say.

DON'T try to find a lesson in the child's death, such as "the purpose of this is to bring your family closer."

DON'T tell them what they should feel or do, as in "You ought to be feeling better by now."

DON'T act superspiritual or as if you know all the answers.

DON'T say, "At least you have your other children" or "You can always have another child." Children are not interchangeable; one cannot replace another.

DON'T make any comments that suggest medical care or other care was in any way lacking; remember that they are already dealing with self-imposed guilt.

2. *For women who are fearful of future pregnancies:* Encourage them to read *The Child Within*—nine months of Bible study for the woman-in-waiting, written by Mari Hanes (Tyndale House Publishers, Inc., Wheaton, Illinois). This helpful book is available through any Christian bookstore.

If medical problems pose a threat in future pregnancies, the closest hospital with a *Neonatal Intensive Care Unit* can provide information concerning recent research in a particular health hazard, as well as the names of physicians who specialize in its treatment.

3. For women who are struggling with infertility and the problems of adoption: Information regarding fertility specialists in your area is available through The American Fertility Society, 1608 13th Avenue South, Birmingham, Alabama 35205.

Books which answer questions about adopting:

Beating the Adoption Game by Cynthia D. Martin (Oak Tree Publications, La Jolla, CA).

A Parent's Guide to Adoption by R. S. Lasnik (Sterling Publishing Company, New York, NY).

National Directory of Intercountry Adoptions (information concerning the adoption of foreign children) from the American Public Welfare Association (U. S. Government Printing Office, Washington, DC).

Adopting the Older Child by C. L. Jewett (Harvard Common Press, Harvard, MA).

Adopting Children with Special Needs by P. J. Kravik (North American Council on Adoptable Children, Riverside, CA).

19 Steps up the Mountain: The Story of the Debolt Family by J. P. Blank (J. B. Lippincott Company, Philadelphia, PA).

A group which provides current national information is:

The Adoption Resource of North America
67 Irving Place
New York, NY

*4. For ministry to women considering
abortion:* No specific details about abortion
were listed in the chapter "The Regret of an
Abortion," because details would have
weighed that chapter down. But at this time
in our society, at least three out of every ten
pregnancies end in abortion. In Washington
State, where I live, there were as many
abortions last year as there were live births.
Statistics are so high nationwide that you will
likely come in contact with women who are
contemplating abortion.

If you know clearly what you believe, and if
you are able to convey that belief graciously
and lovingly on a one-to-one basis, then you
can experience the privilege of saving the life
of a child. You will be fulfilling God's
exhortation to "Speak up for those who cannot
speak for themselves, for the rights of all who
are destitute" (Proverb 31:6, *New International Version*).

First, you must be comfortable with your
knowledge of the Bible's stand on this subject.
If a woman is open to listening to Scripture,
Psalm 139 is an excellent place to begin.
Verses 13-16 deal with God's concern for the
unborn child, and are especially beautiful

when read from *The Living Bible*.

If you are able to share further, there are Scriptures which apply specifically to abortion.

A. Abortion is a sin:

"Neither shall the children be put to death for [the sin of] the fathers . . ." (Deuteronomy 24:16, *KJV*). See also Exodus 21:22, 23.

"Shall I give my first-born for my transgression, the fruit of my body for the sin of my soul?" (Micah 6:7, *KJV*).

B. The fetus is not the mother's property; it belongs to God:

"Whatsoever openeth the womb . . . is mine," says the Lord (Exodus 13:2, *KJV*).

"From my mother's womb you have been my God" (Psalm 22:10, *NIV*).

"Children are a gift from the Lord" (Psalm 127:3, *TLB*).

C. God asks each expectant mother to make the right choice:

"I call heaven and earth to record this day against you, that I have set before you life and death, blessing and cursing: therefore choose life, that both thou and thy seed may live" (Deuteronomy 30:19, *KJV*).

D. God has great love for the helpless:

Deuteronomy 1:39: "I will give the land to

the children they said would die in the wilderness" *(TLB)*.

Jonah 4:11: "And why shouldn't I feel sorry for a great city like Nineveh with its 120,000 people in utter spiritual darkness, and all its cattle?" *(TLB)*.

Note: In this passage from the Book of Jonah, God tells the prophet that he does not want to destroy the wicked city of Nineveh because of the little children, who "don't know their left hand from their right."

Second, you need to be aware of the different abortion procedures:

1. *Dilation and Curettage.* The cervix is dilated with a series of instruments; then the placenta and fetus are scraped from the uterine wall.

2. *Suction Curettage* (vacuum aspiration). The cervix is dilated and a suction machine draws all evidence of the pregnancy from the womb. (The force used is twenty-eight times that of a vacuum cleaner.)

3. *Saline Injection* (salt poisoning). Though outlawed in Japan and other countries because of its inherent risk to the mother, this procedure is used widely in the U.S. for abortions after the sixteenth week from the last menstrual period. A concentrated salt solution is injected into the amniotic fluid. The baby swallows it and usually dies within twenty-four hours.

(Note: the mother then goes through a regular labor, but delivers a dead fetus.)

4. *Hysterotomy.* While similar to the caesarean section, its purpose is to terminate life rather than to save it. This method is used if the saline solution has failed.

"These surgical procedures, often referred to as 'safe and simple,' are not without the risk of serious, life-threatening complications." Imagine the agony experienced by the fetus undergoing these surgical procedures.

CONFUSING QUESTIONS

When I became a Christian and understood the biblical truth that the unborn baby is a person, I knew that for myself abortion was totally out of the question. I believed that it was a sin and that it was wrong in almost every situation. Almost. I was confused because I had heard the proabortionists say, "What about pregnancies that are the result of rape or incest?" I felt such compassion for the woman who might find herself in that situation that I didn't know what to believe.

After I wrote *The Child Within,* I began to come in contact with pregnant teenagers who asked me to help them find Christian homes for their babies. The church we pastored was growing rapidly and as the word got out, more young women were referred to me. Eventually

I was offered a position with our state's WACAP adoption agency, where I have counseled unwed mothers for three years.

In the first year I met several young women who told me that their pregnancies had resulted from rape. But after meeting together, as a trust relationship was developed, each girl confided that she had not been raped but rather was pregnant by a boyfriend. As I talked to social workers in both state and private agencies, I discovered that this information during the counseling experience is fairly common.

But I was prompted to do some research to answer my own question: "How often is pregnancy the result of rape?" The facts I discovered are amazing. There *are* answers to the abortionists' argument that "liberal abortion laws are needed because of rape victims."

Mary Schott Ward, coordinator of the National Organization for Women's Committee on Rape says, "As pro-lifers contend, pregnancy resulting from rape is very rare."

In California in 1970, a mere .07 percent of all abortions were performed because of incest or rape (and statutory, as well as criminal, rape is included in the total).

In a study done in Buffalo, New York, there hasn't been a confirmed pregnancy due to rape in over thirty years.

Over a ten-year period in the Minneapolis/ St. Paul metropolitan area, there were over 3,500 cases of rapes, with zero cases of pregnancy.

The reasons for the absence of pregnancy following rape are many. Often a victim is infertile because of her monthly cycle, or because she is using the pill or other contraceptives. Also, studies indicate a high percentage of sterility and vasectomies, as well as impotency, in the attackers.

Another reason is the effect that fear has on a woman who has been molested. In response to fear, a great deal of adrenaline is produced, which usually interrupts the hormone pattern of a monthly cycle. The absence of the reproductive hormones prevents ovulation and fertilization.

Pregnancy resulting from incest is also rare, and it presents abortionists with a different problem. In my own experience, which is in agreement with available statistics, incest victims usually hide their pregnancies for as long as they are able. They are scared and ashamed, and often do not confide in a school nurse or other adult until they have entered the last trimester. By that time, I believe, the labor pain and trauma involved in a saline abortion is greater than the trauma of carrying the infant a few more weeks to natural delivery. According to the *Abortion Guidelines for the State of New York,*

> The more effective response is to deal with the environment under which the girl is being victimized and provide her with the medical and emotional help she so desperately needs.
>
> The Medical Society of the State of New York would like to caution all physicians that an abortion performed after the twelfth week of gestation is fraught with tremendous danger.

Among the minute percentage of molested women who conceive, there is the life story of Ethel Waters.

She is probably the most famous female soul singer who ever lived. Her career began on Broadway, led to roles in movies such as "Gone with the Wind," and included many concert tours. In her last days, she was a frequent soloist at Billy Graham crusades, performing her favorite hymn, "His Eye Is on the Sparrow."

Ethel Waters was born as the result of the rape of a thirteen-year-old black girl by a mulatto neighbor. In her lifetime Ethel Waters accomplished a great deal and helped many people.

"Long ago I learned the verse that says God's eye is on the sparrow," she shared, "and

I took as my own the following verse that says, 'Fear not . . . you are of more value than many sparrows.' "

What About the Pregnancy That Endangers the Life of the Mother? Another amazing truth is that, because of medical advances, pregnancy almost never threatens the life of the mother. Dr. Alan Guttmacher, the author of noted textbooks on gynecology, states that "there are no situations today in which the mother's life can't be saved without taking the baby's."

Dr. Guttmacher says that the one exception is what is termed *ectopic* (from the Greek *ek*, "out of," and *topos*, "place"), or *tubular pregnancy.* This occurs when an egg begins to develop in the Fallopian tube rather than in the flexible uterus. An ectopic pregnancy simply cannot produce a live child. Therefore, the operation is considered major abdominal surgery and not an abortion. The condition would cause the Fallopian tube to rupture and would almost invariably kill the mother.

Other Problems. For an inspiring story about a problem pregnancy, read *Walking through the Fire* by Laurel Lee. You may wish to purchase printed material which can be given to the expectant mother.

Realize that the most common reason for abortion is that the young woman does not know there are alternatives. An expectant teenager may need help finding a supportive foster home. She may not know that if she chooses to place the child, all her medical costs will be covered. An older woman may need help in finding a maternity home. She may need encouragement in contacting government agencies which offer helpful programs. Most communities now offer special childbirth training courses for the unmarried mother. If yours does not, perhaps you can help to get one started.

Getting involved is not easy. It takes courage, and it means hard work. But Christ's Word to you is: "Inasmuch as ye have done it unto one of the least of these my brethren, ye have done it unto me" (Matthew 25:40, *KJV*).

There may be times, however, when a woman you have talked with still chooses an abortion.

How should you react in that situation?

When a young girl whom I had counseled chose an abortion, I was deeply grieved. But I was certain of one thing—I could not now reject her. She still needed my friendship, perhaps more than ever.

Pastor Jack Hayford teaches his congregation a set of biblical principles which give excellent guidelines for dealing with the multi-faceted issues of unplanned pregnancy:

1. A life exists at conception.
2. Sin abounding takes its toll.
3. Grace abounding covers sin (Romans 5:20).
4. Faith can overcome trial.
5. Love covers a multitude of sin.
6. Believers can help provide some answers.
7. We don't know all the answers (see 1 Corinthians 13:9-12).

Pastor Hayford adds:

"We want to maintain Bible standards, not proposing sloppy morality or situation ethics. But neither do we want to be bracketed with those who exude self-righteousness with trite slogans. We want to minister grace and forgiveness."

When Jesus walked this earth, he met people where they were and then led them on to wholeness. As his representatives, we must do the same.

In my experience as a social worker and pastor's wife, I have seen many well-meaning Christians attempt to counsel, and, unknowingly, talk from a spiritually superior attitude to a woman who has had an abortion or to a grieving sister whose faith was shaky. People often are not at our own level of spiritual knowledge, but "the mind of Christ" that the Book of Philippians exhorts us to have is an attitude of humility and compassion.

One of the most precious descriptions of the Messiah's work in a life is found in Isaiah 42:3: "A bruised reed shall he not break, and the smoking flax shall he not quench: he shall bring forth judgment unto truth" *(KJV)*. In other words, we do not want to quench the smallest hope or flicker of faith, but instead, to fan it into a warm, enduring flame.

Together, we are exhorted to answer the call of God: *We speak for children yet unborn.* Proverbs 31:8—"You should defend those who cannot help themselves" *(TLB)*.

We speak for women who have no knowledge of God's will as shown in his Word. Isaiah 62:1—"For Zion's sake will I not hold my peace, and for Jerusalem's sake I will not rest, until the righteousness thereof go forth as brightness, and the salvation thereof as a lamp that burneth" *(KJV)*.

We speak to those in the midst of grief. Isaiah 61:1—"The Spirit of the Lord is upon me; because the Lord hath anointed me to preach good tidings unto the meek; he hath sent me to bind up the brokenhearted, to proclaim liberty to the captives, and the opening of the prison to them that are bound" *(KJV)*.

To women experiencing pain and grief associated with abortion, miscarriage, still-birth, or infertility, there is an answer. It is Christ's love, which offers strength and hope. Are you committed to answer God's call: "Comfort ye, my people"? Are you ready to be his channel of love and help lead women beyond heartache?

The magnitude of our task need not discourage us. In a 1982 CBS-TV interview, Nobel Peace Prize winner Mother Teresa was asked about her work in India: "Your Sisters of Mercy must sometimes grow very dis-couraged," the reporter commented, "because no matter how many they save, there are multitudes left untouched in the vast popula-tion of India."

Mother Teresa's answer was a jewel of godly wisdom. "Oh, no!" she said. "You see, I do not count as you count. I count the way God counts. Not by thousands. By *ones*. The ones we have touched. . . . There is no way to describe the way God sees the value of one."

BIBLIOGRAPHY

Briggs, Dorothy Corkille. *Your Child's Self-Esteem.* New York: Doubleday, 1978.

Dobelis, Inge N. (editor). *The Family Legal Guide.* Pleasantville, New York: Reader's Digest Association, 1981.

Freiling, Edward, PhD. *The Position of Modern Science on the Beginning of Human Life.* Greystone, Virginia: Sun Life, 1979.

Gardner, R. F. *Abortion: The Personal Dilemma.* Old Tappan, New Jersey: Fleming H. Revell Company, 1974.

Howard, Ted and Rifkin, Jeremy. *Who Should Play God?* New York: Dell Publishing, 1977.

Knaack, Twila. *Ethel Waters: I Touched a Sparrow.* Waco, Texas: Word Books, 1978.

Liley, Dr. H. M. I. *Modern Motherhood.* New York: Random House, 1969.

Martin, Cynthia D. *Beating the Adoption Game.* La Jolla, California: Oak Tree Publications, 1980.

McCleary, Elliott H., *New Miracles of Childbirth.* New York: McKay Company, 1974.

Menning, Barbara Eck. *Infertility: A Guide for the Childless Couple.* Englewood Cliffs, New Jersey: Prentice-Hall, 1977.

Miller, Madeline S. and J. Lane. *Harper's Encyclopedia of Bible Life* (revised). San Francisco: Harper and Row, 1978.

Odell, Catherine and William. *The First Human Right: A Pro-Life Primer*. Huntington, Indiana: OSV Inc., 1983.

Pizer, Hank and Palinski, Christine O'Brien. *Coping with a Miscarriage*. New York: Dial Press, 1980.

Strong, James. *Strong's Exhaustive Concordance of the Bible* (revised). New York: Abingdon, 1974.

Unger, Merrill and White, William. *Expository Dictionary of the Old Testament,* Nashville: Thomas Nelson Inc., 1980.

Vine, W. E. *An Expository Dictionary of New Testament Words.* Old Tappan, New Jersey: Fleming H. Revell Company, 1940.